START AND RUN A PROFITABLE HOME DAY CARE

START AND RUN A PROFITABLE HOME DAY CARE
Your step-by-step business plan

Catherine M. Pruissen

Self-Counsel Press
(a division of)
International Self-Counsel Press Ltd.
Canada   U.S.A.

Printed in Canada

First edition: October, 1993

Canadian Cataloguing in Publication Data
    Pruissen, Catherine M. (Catherine Mary), 1957–
    Start and Run a profitable home day care

    (Self-counsel business series)
    Includes bibliographical references.
    ISBN 0-88908-294-4

    1. Day care centers — Management. I. Title.
II. Series.
HV851.P78 1993   362. 7′12′068   C93-091592-5

Cover photography by Terry Guscott, ATN Visuals, Vancouver, B.C.

Self-Counsel Press
(a division of)
International Self-Counsel Press Ltd.

1481 Charlotte Road
North Vancouver, British Columbia
V7J 1H1

1704 N. State Street
Bellingham, Washington
98225

To Candace and Daniel, you are my inspiration.

CONTENTS

TABLES

WORKSHEETS

SAMPLES

ACKNOWLEDGMENTS

I would like to acknowledge the many organizations, licensing offices, and resource personnel who responded generously to my requests for information, information, information. Their overwhelming support and offers to be of assistance were greatly appreciated.

To Helene Sallans, your words of wisdom mean so much.

To my children, Candace and Daniel, who endured my writing and researching madness with great patience and understanding.

To my dear friend Colleen, whose friendship I regretfully placed on hold so that I could finish this book on schedule. Your understanding means so much.

INTRODUCTION

When I first considered the idea of writing a book on running a day care, I thought I knew enough about the subject to make writing a book a piece of cake. Well, I was very much misinformed.

This book is the result of much research, much reading, and much learning. But as you'll see when you begin your journey through its pages, child care is a fascinating occupation. The rewards of working with children greatly surpass any of the trials and tribulations you may encounter as you establish your home day care.

One of the most difficult parts of providing child care is keeping track of and conforming to the many rules and regulations. They cover everything from conducting a pre-admission interview with parents to sanitizing your food preparation and diapering areas. Some may appear to be frivolous and time-consuming, but they are all necessary, for you will be providing care for one of life's most precious treasures, children. These youngsters are at our mercy, for they cannot look after themselves and many are too young even to tell us what they need. It is society's duty to establish guidelines that will protect children and ensure that their needs are being met in a safe manner while they are learning to become independent individuals through their physical, intellectual, social, and emotional development.

Although the task of providing quality day care may seem overwhelming, this book will help you lay the foundation for success. Within these pages are ideas for planning your program, activities to stimulate a child's mind and develop physical and social skills, menus to keep the children healthy, and samples of every form and worksheet you will need to get your home day care up and running. Most of all you'll learn everything it takes to obtain your license.

What I hope you learn from this book, above all else, is the importance of providing quality child care. This cannot be measured by the profits you record in your ledger, but in the smiles and happy faces of the children who are growing in all areas of their development thanks to your commitment to provide them with nothing but the best. In the words of Helene Sallans, a former day-care director, "The children must come first and foremost. Children are only children for a very short time and will remember the majority of what goes on in their young lives. What you do with that child in the first five years shapes him or her. As a provider, you play a very big role in that child's life. He or she should be allowed to have opinions and to learn by trial and error. After all, children are really only little people."

Little people indeed, and they need you, as do the many, many families who are struggling to find quality child care. In Canada, there are only enough licensed child-care spaces to serve 1 of every 13 children. The situation in the United States is much the same. So, as you journey through the pages of this book, I hope you find the guidance, the confidence, and the encouragement you need to establish your own home day care. I wish you every success in your endeavor.

Duck, Duck, Goose

This game is great for a group of six to eight children, but it works with larger groups as well.

Object of the game: to stop the fox from getting back to the hole.

How to Play: one child is the "Fox." He or she goes around the outside of a circle of seated children and taps each one on the head and says "Duck." If the Fox says "Goose," then that child chases the Fox around the circle and tries to catch him before the Fox sits in the vacant spot. If the Fox is caught, the Goose goes back to his or her spot and the Fox continues around the circle until he or she is caught. If the Goose does not catch the Fox, that child becomes the new Fox and the game starts over.

1

IS CHILD CARE FOR YOU?

Herbert Hoover once said, "Children are our most valuable natural resource." They are, in fact, our next world leaders. The love, the spirit, the zest for life, the quest for knowledge, and the respect for every living thing they learn from us today will govern all their tomorrows and shape the future for generations to come. With the ever-increasing pressure on women to work outside the home, much of what our children are learning about themselves and the world at large is coming from the nurturing and understanding of loving child-care providers.

It takes a certain kind of person to undertake such a task. This chapter will help you decide if you are that kind of person.

a. THE ENTREPRENEURIAL SPIRIT

Setting up your home to provide care for children can be the road to independence. While people may have many reasons for opening their own business, the quest to be their own boss usually tops that list. Self-employment and the personal freedom it allows is a cherished dream for many people. But that dream, that longing to succeed, that urge to strike out on your own, can become a reality. No matter where you live in North America, there are parents who need someone to provide care for their children.

It is estimated that in Canada in 1990, there were 3,000,000 children under the age of 12 whose mothers worked outside the home. Yet, there were only 321,000 licensed child-care spaces. In the United States, it is estimated that 8,000,000 children under 13 are currently in need of some form of child care. When you also consider that, according to the Child Care Action Campaign (CCAC), —

- 51% of all mothers return to work before their child's first birthday, and

- 23% of all jobs created in the next decade will need to be filled by women, most of whom will become mothers,

there is definitely room for more quality day-care facilities.

Getting your dream out of the shadows and into the "open for business" spotlight is going to take a lot of planning, training, and sheer determination. In this book, I'll show you how to get there. Before we get started, however, you'll want to be absolutely certain that the business of caring for children is really for you.

b. THE BUSINESS OF CHILD CARE

Make no mistake about it. Opening a day care will require an investment, but it will be an investment in you and in your dreams. If you plan to open a home day care, your investment may be more in time than money, although you'll still need to purchase equipment, advertise, and perhaps take training courses or renovate areas of your home.

If you are interested in an out-of-home day-care center, your expenses will be much greater: rent, renovations, large equipment purchases, staff, and extensive advertising.

Unlike parents who work a standard eight-hour shift, your days are likely to include many twelve-hour shifts. If a desperate parent calls to say he or she is stranded with a flat tire on the freeway and will be late picking Janey up, you can't simply say "Sorry, I shut up shop at 5 p.m. You'll find Janey waiting for you somewhere out on the street." You have the responsibility to look after the child, no matter how late the parent or how urgent your own appointment.

As an entrepreneur, you'll find yourself resembling Bartholomew Cubbins in the Dr. Seuss tale *The 500 Hats of Bartholomew Cubbins;* you'll be wearing a new hat every time you turn around. From the moment you open your doors, you'll be owner, cook, bottle washer, diaper changer, storyteller, maintenance person, bookkeeper, advertising consultant, inventory clerk, parent counselor, administrator, and much, much more.

You can rest assured that at some point it will seem overwhelming. The hours are long, stress is ever-present, recognition for this type of work may seem nonexistent, and quite often finding the stamina and ingenuity to entertain children all day requires real dedication. But to anyone who values the innocence, wonder, and unconditional love of children, this line of work can be a source of pride and pleasure as well as income.

c. WHY DAY CARE?

There are as many reasons for opening one's door to day care as there are providers. The most common reason is that a parent wants to be home with his or her own children while still contributing to the family budget. Other day-care providers want playmates for their children or want to enhance their children's social development.

You can feel good about offering a community service desperately needed by many parents in your neighborhood who are searching for long-lasting, quality care for their children. Running your own business and providing a necessary service can give you a feeling of accomplishment and build your self-esteem.

Whatever your reasons, you must realize that the service you provide will have a profound impact on the lives of young children at a time when they are most vulnerable. It is during the first three years of life that a child develops emotionally. Young children need to be held, cuddled, played with, and talked to. By fulfilling these emotional needs as well as taking care of the basic physical needs to be fed, dry, and comfortable, you will build a foundation for "your" children that will enhance their later skills and relationships.

There will be many rewards for you as a child-care provider. Each will make your work treasurable, memorable. In the words of Helene Sallans, a former day-care director, "My greatest success is when we had the children from infancy right up to school age, and they went away and came back just to visit. You know you've been successful when a child wants to return."

d. EVALUATING YOURSELF AND YOUR SITUATION

Before you begin your journey through this book to learn the practical skills of child care, you must evaluate honestly your personality, your character, and your ability to handle this program. To do this, use the three-step plan outlined below.

Step one is a self-evaluation to help you learn if you have what it takes to work with children on a daily basis.

WORKSHEET #1
CHILD-CARE PROVIDER'S SELF-EVALUATION QUIZ

QUESTION:	YES	NO	SOMETIMES
1. I am in good health and have lots of energy.			
2. I have a genuine love for children and enjoy being around them.			
3. I enjoy thinking of new games and things to do with children.			
4. I am organized enough to keep financial records.			
5. I am good with people and can get along with most everyone.			
6. I have the ability to work cooperatively with parents and to listen to their ideas on how they raise their children.			
7. I am not afraid to discuss problems and to state my point of view.			
8. I am willing to give my day-care program three years of complete dedication.			
9. I can handle a child's tantrums and spilled milk diplomatically.			
10. I enjoy physical contact and am not afraid to hug, touch, or cuddle a child.			
11. I can handle the stress of children tugging at me ceaselessly all day.			
12. I am easygoing, pleasant, warm, and affectionate.			
13. I am willing to learn about child development, health, and nutrition.			
14. I am organized enough to handle a number of staff and related problems.			
15. I am quick and sensible when emergencies arise.			
16. I am willing to comply with licensing standards and regulations and will aim at providing the best possible care.			
17. I am safety conscious.			

QUESTION:	YES	NO	SOMETIMES
18. I am not unnerved by messes and welcome a child's active play.			
19. I am flexible enough to allow deviations from the structures of a program.			
20. I have a positive attitude towards life.			
21. I have a good sense of humor.			
22. I am motivated and consider myself to be a high achiever.			
23. I am receptive to different methods of discipline.			
24. I am willing to invite parents to stay for coffee or welcome their after-hour calls when they have concerns.			

Step two is a family evaluation to help you determine how your decision to provide day care will effect the lives of your family.

Step three will be to address the other concerns that will affect your decision, such as licensing, training, zoning regulations, and even your neighbors.

1. Step one: self-evaluation

Take the Self-evaluation Quiz in Worksheet #1 to see just how well you are suited to a career in child care. Remember, it is more important to answer the questions honestly than to try to deceive yourself into believing you possess every one of these qualities.

To answer yes to every question on the quiz, you would have to be superhuman, the type of person we all wish we were. What you will gain from this evaluation is the realization that there is no perfect care-giver, just as there are no perfect children

and no perfect parents. This realization will help you deal with children and their short-comings in a very positive way, for we are, none of us, angels.

If you answered no or sometimes to questions 2, 10, 11, or 18, this should be a good indicator of your honest feelings about children. If you are not genuinely fond of children and have little patience for their foibles, you should consider carefully whether caring for children on a daily basis is something you are emotionally equipped to do.

If you answered no or sometimes to questions 3, 4, 13, 14, or 17, you may need to upgrade your skills in these areas. Books on child development, health, nutrition, safety, games and activities for children, as well as accounting and recordkeeping are available at your local library. See the Bibliography at the back of the book for a list of titles. Courses on all these subjects may also be offered at your local community college.

If you answered no or sometimes to questions 5, 6, 7, 9, and 19, you should consider getting some extra help developing your people skills. To run a successful day care, you'll have to be able to assert yourself, resolve conflicts, and negotiate compromises in as businesslike a way as possible. You can't let your personal feelings about your clients or the way they raise their children affect your ability to offer good service. In the child-care business, communication and a positive attitude toward your work are essential to providing quality care. If you simply can't get along with parents or respect their choices for their children, perhaps you should consider another line of work.

Your temperament is another aspect of your personality that plays an important role in your ability to offer quality day care. If you answered no or sometimes to questions 12, 15, 20, 21, or 22, then this could indicate that you are of a somewhat anxious disposition and not suited to handling children. Children are as unpredictable as the weather. You should consider whether you can handle the stress.

For you to consider a career in child care, it is essential that you scored at least 17 yes answers. Ideally, your remaining 8 responses would be sometimes. Too many no answers should sound a warning bell that perhaps you would be better suited to another profession.

As a bit of added insurance, you might want to do volunteer work in a day-care center. Most of these facilities will welcome your help and the experience will give you a better indication as to whether you are really suited to a career in day care.

The one thing most successful caregivers have in common is their love for children and their desire to make a difference. Mixed in with these characteristics is a certain amount of inner calm, strength of character, and an ability to work through an array of problems like frustration, loneliness, and temper tantrums.

2. Step two: family evaluation

As a child-care provider, you will be the role model for the children who will look to you for all their needs. Your ability to be flexible, loving, and understanding of their individuality will help them grow into well-adjusted human beings. In order to foster a child's emotional and intellectual growth, you will need the support of the other members of your family. Their support and willingness to help out can make a big difference in how you feel about the work you choose to do and how you care for the children. When your spouse gripes about the toys on the floor or your school-age daughter insists on your undivided attention, the tension will affect the type of care you provide.

To help you consider issues related to your family, complete the Family Evaluation Quiz (see Worksheet #2). You might want to consider making photocopies of this quiz for each member of your family old enough to read and answer the questions. Their answers might be quite different from what you would guess. For younger children, take the time to sit down with them and discuss the questions that concern them. This will give you a good picture of how your family feels.

Don't let all these questions kill your desire to open your home and your heart to children. There are many ways to help your family adjust. Consider carefully the answers to the quiz and you can begin to think of how to deal with any potential problems.

To gather some ideas, you might want to visit with other day-care providers in your area and discuss your concerns. Take your children with you so they can see how well other children get along and how much fun they have. Take your spouse along on one of these visits as well, so he or she can see just how your plans will affect the way things are in your home.

WORKSHEET #2
FAMILY EVALUATION QUIZ

1. How will your decision to open your door to child care affect your family?

2. Will your spouse help out during his or her off hours?

3. How does he or she feel about your decision to welcome children into your home?

4. Will your children welcome the noise and toys and will they help you entertain the youngsters?

5. How will your decision affect your family scheduling?

6. Will your children be willing to share "Mommy" with the other children?

7. How will your family feel about your re-arranging the house to provide for adequate play space and an assortment of toys and books?

8. How about your finances? Will establishing a home day care drain your family's cash reserve?

9. How much is your family willing to allow you to invest? Will it be enough?

10. Can the remaining money sustain your current lifestyle until you are on your feet and making a profit?

11. If adjustments are to be made, exactly how willing is the rest of the family to making the adjustments?

12. When your own child gets ill, will you feel comfortable having other children around when your child needs your attention?

13. If you have family pets, how will they fit into your plans?

14. If you want to open a day-care centre away from home, how will your time away from home affect your family?

If scheduling is going to be a problem, you may be able to set your hours to work around your family. For example, you might accept children only after your spouse has gone to work. Offer to pay your teenager to help you play with the children when he or she comes home from school. Enlist the help of your youngsters by asking them to show the new children around your home or facility and to introduce them to the other children. Allow them to help you feed the babies and prepare the lunch or snacks.

Your children will have to adjust to a great many things, such as allowing other children to play with their toys or not being able to sit on Mommy's lap all the time like they used to. They may even find themselves having to share your lap with another baby who also requires your attention. How will you handle what could be a very upsetting situation for your child?

Helping your young children adjust to strange children playing with their toys will take some effort and understanding. Talking to other providers will give you some ideas on handling jealousies while teaching sharing and other social issues. Consider locking your child's favorite toys away while the visiting children are present. When the company leaves, your child will be able to play with these toys without having to relinquish sole possession of them.

If your older children have concerns about "private space," you could establish a quiet or rest space for them. For example, your program could be designed so that the TV room/den is off-limits for the visiting children after 3 p.m. so that your children may study or relax there, away from the hustle and bustle.

My son had not yet been born when I took in my first child-care child. My daughter, who was just over a year old, welcomed a new playmate. By the time her brother came along, she was already used to having another child in her world and she welcomed

his arrival. The biggest adjustment I faced was helping the little one I cared for to welcome not only the newest member of my family, but each new member of our extended family. She was an only child and to help her cope, I had many discussions with her while we played. We talked about sharing and how we would all have to get along if our time together was to be fun. It was that time we shared that helped her to adjust.

Even now, my eldest watches carefully the attention I give to the two-year-old I have in my care. I have to be careful to include her in the things we do. She is more than willing to fetch a stuffed toy or to help with the potty training, but she is also quick to snatch a hug from me when the little guy wanders off on his own.

3. Step three: situation evaluation

I call this the food-for-thought category. It is in no way intended to deter you from following your dream or to make you nervous. It's just that the more you understand about what you are getting involved in, the easier it will be for you to succeed.

To help you start thinking about the wide variety of issues you should consider, complete the Situation Evaluation Quiz (see Worksheet #3).

If zoning or other restrictions absolutely rule out the possibility of running a day care in your home, your only options are moving or opening an out-of-home day care. On the other hand, if the renovations your home would require to make it safe and workable as a day-care home are large and costly, you'll have to decide if your business is worth it.

For example, it will be difficult to entertain a group of children indoors when it is sunny and pleasant outside. Do you have an outdoor space for the children? If your yard is not fenced, you may be looking at a serious safety issue and one that could cost a lot to remedy; fencing is not cheap.

8

WORKSHEET #3
SITUATION EVALUATION QUIZ

1. Do zoning restrictions in your area make running a business from home difficult or impossible?

2. Is there anything in the day-care licensing requirements for your area that would make it difficult for you to obtain a license?

3. Do you have the space to entertain several active children, both indoors and out?

4. Do you have a fenced yard?

5. What will you do if you become ill with the flu or a bad cold or perhaps something worse?

6. Is there someone you can hire to help you through the holiday times and the sick times?

7. Are you willing to look after an ill child and at which point would you prefer the parent take the child home?

8. What about vacations — yours and the families you provide care for?

9. What about the days when your school will be closed and your children will be hanging around? How will you handle the extra workload?

10. Are you willing to study towards obtaining a certificate in early childhood education or child development?

11. How do my neighbors feel about having a day care next door?

To accommodate your new business, your home will undergo a variety of changes, particularly if you no longer have young children scampering about. With careful planning, you can arrange your home to suit an assortment of toys, books, child-sized tables and chairs, as well as spaces for active play and rest. You'll need toilet-training supplies and diaper-changing areas. Comfort and space, especially for crawling babies and toddlers on the go will be a major concern. Planning for messy activities and free play will take considerable thought.

You will need to childproof your home by installing electrical outlet covers, locking up all cleaning supplies and medicines, and by keeping lamp and appliance cords out of a child's reach. How far are you willing to go to meet the necessary safety regulations imposed by your local and state or provincial licensing boards?

Not all families will be able to or even want to schedule their holidays to correspond to yours. How will you handle this?

Many provincial and state day-care licensing boards now require successful completion of a course of studies in early childhood education. Consider whether you have the time and money to take such a course.

After researching the zoning laws, municipal bylaws, business restrictions, and possibly even your home-owner's association covenant, which may exclude home child-care programs, you may also want to discuss your plans with many of your neighbors. There may be someone in your neighborhood who opposes your plans because they do not want the extra noise, traffic, or persons using their parking spaces. When talking to the neighbors about your proposal, assure them you will honestly work toward avoiding any unnecessary problems and that you'll welcome hearing from them about any of their concerns. You might even consider having an open house for your neighbors to come in and visit with you and the children to see how you operate, and, if appropriate, to accept their suggestions.

Banana Pops

Cut, peel and halve bananas. Insert a skewer into each banana section.

Freeze for 30 minutes.

In a blender finely chop
peanuts or pecans
or graham crackers.

Melt in a tall narrow container
12 oz. chocolate chips
1 oz. butter
¼ cup hot water.

- Place container in a saucepan half filled with water; heat to melt chips.
- Dip frozen bananas into chocolate sauce.
- Roll into either finely chopped nuts or graham crackers.
- Place Banana Pops on a tray covered with wax paper.
- Freeze for 1 hour.

2

ASSESSING THE NEED FOR CHILD CARE

So you've determined that you are the right type of person to open a day care and you understand beyond a shadow of a doubt that it's going to take a lot of hard work. Great! Now you should assess the need for child care in your area. It is fruitless for you to go to all the trouble and expense of planning and setting up a day care only to discover your area doesn't require your services.

a. DETERMINING YOUR OBJECTIVES

Your objectives in assessing your community's child-care needs will include identifying —

(a) what age groups are most in need of care,

(b) how many parents are on waiting lists with other facilities,

(c) how many parents working in local businesses might be interested in your services, and

(d) what type of care these parents need.

You can be even more specific with your objectives if you want. For example, if you are only interested in caring for children under two years old, your objective would be to find out how many parents in your area with children in the under-two range require child care, or how many infants are on waiting lists at local centers.

b. CREATING A QUESTIONNAIRE

Once you know what kind of information you want, you can create a list of questions designed to collect that information. Sample #1 shows a typical child-care needs assessment questionnaire. Adapt your list of questions to obtain the information you want. For example, instead of asking what ages of children might need day care, you could ask if the respondent has or will have any children under two in need of day care, if that is the age group you are focusing on.

Be sure to include a space for respondents to give their names and addresses, if they choose, as shown at the bottom of Sample #1. This will give you a list of potential customers when you open for business.

c. COLLECTING THE DATA

There are several ways to collect the data you need, including —

(a) mailed questionnaires,

(b) telephone interviews, and

(c) in-person interviews door-to-door or at local shopping centers.

1. Mailed questionnaires

Mailing out questionnaires along with a cover letter such as the one shown in Sample #2 is one way to collect your information. You could choose to mail to everyone within a certain geographic area (such as

SAMPLE #1
CHILD-CARE NEEDS ASSESSMENT QUESTIONNAIRE*

1. Do you think our community has adequate child-care spaces?
   Yes_____ No_____ Don't know_____

2. Do you currently have children under the age of 12 living at home?
   Yes_____ No_____

3. Are any of your children currently in day care?
   Yes_____ No_____

4. What are the ages of your children who are currently in day care?
   Child 1_____ Child 2_____ Child 3_____

5. Are you satisfied with your child-care arrangements?

6. Who provides your current day care arrangements?
   _____family member, nanny, or in-home caregiver
   _____caregiver outside the home
   _____child-care center
   _____nursery school
   _____other (please describe)_____

7. What is your general need for child care?
   Months   J   F   M   A   M   J
              J   A   S   O   N   D

   Days   S   M   T   W   T   F   S

   Hours _____

*These questions are based on the SAMPLE QUESTIONNAIRES BOOKLET, produced by the Childcare Resource and Research Unit. Reproduced with the permission of the Childcare Resource and Research Unit, Centre for Urban and Community Studies, University of Toronto, Toronto, Ontario.

8. What fees do you currently pay for child care?

$_____per week

9. Would you be willing to pay a higher fee to have more satisfactory child-care arrangements?

Yes_____ No_____ Unsure_____

10. Are your child-care fees subsidized by the government?

Yes_____ No_____

11. If your child is in school, what arrangements do you make for holidays and teacher professional development days?

_____no special arrangements

_____special arrangements for some days

_____special arrangements for all days

12. What are your arrangements?

_____you take time off from work

_____your spouse or partner takes time off

_____friend or relative provides care in your home

_____friend or relative provides care in their home

_____other (please describe)_____

13. Would you prefer to have your children in a facility close to where you work?

Yes_____ No_____ Doesn't matter_____

14. Do you live in _____ community?

Yes_____ No_____

15. Do you work or study in _____ community?

Yes_____ No_____

16. Do you plan to return to work in the near future?

    Yes_____ No_____

17. Do you feel you will be in need of day care in the near future?

    Yes_____ No_____

18. What are the ages of your children who will require care?

    _____0 - 6 months

    _____6 months - 1 year

    _____1 - 2 years

    _____2 - 3 years

    _____3 - 4 years

    _____4 years +

19. If finances and availability were not a problem, what type of child-care arrange-
    ments would you prefer? Please pick three, listing your choices in order: 1 - first,
    2 - second, and 3 - third

    _____day-care center

    _____regulated private home day care

    _____parent/child drop-in program

    _____child drop-off center for occasional use

    _____nursery school

    _____trained caregiver for occasional use

    _____play school

20. If you are expecting your first child or planning to adopt your first child within
    the next year, please answer the following:

    If money and availability were no problem, what type of child-care arrange-
    ments would you choose. Pick three and rank in order of preference.

    _____child care in your home

    _____regulated care in a caregiver's home

    _____unregulated care in a caregiver's home

    _____child-care center

_____nursery school
_____after-school program in child's school
_____other _____ (please describe)

If you have any other comments or concerns about your child-care arrangements, please feel free to note them here:

If you are interested in the results of this survey, or would like to be informed about any new facilities opening in your community, please include the following:

Name:
Address:
Phone:
Postal/Zip code

COVER LETTER FOR QUESTIONNAIRE

Dear Community Members,

I am conducting a survey to assess the child care needs in the community area. It is my desire to establish a family day home or child care center in the area, and therefore, I need to know how many parents would be interested in a new facility. Would you please complete the appropriate portions of the questionnaire and mail it back to me as soon as possible in the attached, self-addressed, stamped envelope.

The information will be held in strict confidence. Your help is greatly appreciated, and I thank you.

Sincerely,

Mary Stewart

---

within five miles of your home), or do a random sampling (one in ten homes) over a wider area.

Mailing questionnaires is easy, but it may not be the best way to gather information. Many people will simply toss your questionnaire aside as "junk mail" when it appears in their mail box. Even those with some interest in the matter and every intention of returning your questionnaire may forget to do so. Therefore, your response rate will be quite low. The mail is also expensive, particularly when you factor in the low response rate (see section **d.** below).

To encourage a better response rate, you might employ a few of the following techniques:

(a) Keep track of where you mailed the questionnaires and, after a certain period of time, visit the homes in person to collect the completed questionnaires.

(b) Attach a self-addressed, stamped envelope to each questionnaire (even more expensive, of course).

(c) Place a small ad in your community newsletter or on a local bulletin board requesting all questionnaires be returned by a certain date.

2. Telephone interviews

Telephone interviews have the advantage of creating direct, immediate contact with your information source. You will get a better response rate than through a mail-out. Telephoning is also cheaper than mailing. In addition, you get a chance to give a great first impression of your business by coming across as professional, efficient, and eager to provide good service. But don't try to "sell" your business at this stage; that comes later. Right now, you should simply identify yourself as representing the XYZ Day Care and say that you are doing some market research.

The disadvantage of telephone research for some people is that they feel uncomfortable telephoning strangers and asking them to answer questions. In addition, you may find that many people have become hostile to telephone solicitation and are immediately on guard when approached by telephone.

Your own nervousness will become less the more telephone calls you make and you should be able to handle any of the respondent's hostility by assuring him or her that you are not selling anything, but are merely doing research. Consider doing telephone research as good practice for your diplomacy and people skills, both of which you will need once you open your home day care!

Your telephone is also your free ticket to a number of other information sources. One of your first calls should be to your local day-care resource and referral agency. This agency can tell you what type of care is needed where you live. You should also contact your local social services office, elementary school, or parent advisory council for similar information.

Telephone the personnel departments of local industries, large businesses, or hospitals to inquire about the number of parents who are looking for child care. You can also contact your regional planning agency to see if any surveys have been done regarding the need for child care in your region.

Combine these resources with a call to other child-care facilities and you should be able to get a pretty good indication of the need for child care where you live.

3. In-person interviews

Another way to collect data is to approach people in person, either at their door or in streets, parking lots, or shopping centers. (You may need the permission of the property manager before stopping people on privately owned property such as malls.)

Once you have approached someone, you could either hand out a questionnaire with a request for return by mail, ask the person to complete the questionnaire while you wait, or simply ask him or her to answer the questions verbally while you note down the answers.

Obviously, in-person interviews require even more self-confidence than telephoning. However, people are less likely to rudely walk away from you than to hang up the phone.

d. ESTIMATING COSTS

Once you have decided how you will go about collecting your information, you'll want to estimate the cost needs of your assessment, most of which will be determined by the method and scale of your research. You should have a budget for this market research and adjust your research to fit within that budget.

For example, you might decide that you can afford to spend $200 on market research. So, if you do a mail-out, you need to include the cost of printing the questionnaire, envelopes, and postage (and return envelopes and postage, if you choose to include those). Add to this the cost of your time spent —

- developing the questionnaire,
- addressing the envelopes,
- stuffing the envelopes, and
- attaching the postage.

Printing — 200 4-page questionnaires $40

Envelopes — 200 @ 9¢   18

Postage — 200 @ 50¢   100

Development — 2 hours @ $6   12

Addressing — 3 hours @ $6   18

Stuffing — 2 hours @ $6   12

Attaching postage — 2 hours @ $6   12

TOTAL $212

This is fairly close to your original budget of $200, so you might think this is fine. However, you still have to look at your response rate, which is, after all, the important thing. So, with a mail-out of 200, and a response rate of 5% or 1 in 20 (a good response rate), you can expect a response of 10. Aside from the fact that a response of 10 is not very useful for any kind of statistical analysis, you are paying $21.20 for each response.

Now let's look at a telephone campaign. You may estimate each response call will take you 13 minutes and for every response call, you will have to go through four 30-second non-response calls. To get 100 responses, then, you will need to spend 100 x 13 minutes + 100 x 4 x 30 seconds or a total of 25 hours. Then you need to figure in the cost of developing your questionnaire and printing it (so you can simply check off the answers as the respondents talk).

Development — 2 hours @ $6	$12
Printing — 100 4-page questionnaires	$20
Interviewing — 25 hours @ $6	$150
TOTAL	$182

Fine, you're under your budget. Now, for your $182, you are getting 100 responses, a much better data base and at a cost of only $1.82 per response.

Of course, if you don't have 25 hours to spend telephoning people, the costs of a mail-out may be your only choice. If you value your time higher than $6 per hour, again, the costs of telephoning go higher and the difference between a mail and telephone campaign lessens. You will have to decide how much time and money you have to budget for your market research.

e. ANALYZING YOUR DATA

How you tabulate the results of your research is as important as the questions you asked and the response rate you received. Accuracy and consistency are the important factors in this step of your needs assessment.

Tabulating is most easily done on a computer using a software package designed to manipulate data. Those who are computer shy can manually chart out their results. For example, for a question wherein you asked the ages of the children for whom care was needed, you could tabulate the results under the headings of ages 0 to 6 months, 6 months to 1 year, 1 to 2 years, etc.

It would be fairly easy to tell from your tabulated results just how many children are in need of child care, or how many parents working in the business district would prefer to place their children in a facility close to their place of employment. By reviewing the results of your questions on what families are willing to pay for child care you will have an indication of what rates you should charge. To confirm this, you might consider calling other centers in your area to inquire about their rates.

If your analysis shows a strong need for a particular type of care, you might consider focusing on this area. Even if you are set on looking after three- and four-year-olds, if the need is in infant care, that is the focus most likely to guarantee success. If parents in the vicinity of a particular elementary school are desperate to find after-school care by someone who will take the kids to school and pick them up afterward, you might want to take that on.

Ring-Around-The-Rosy

Any size group will do for this game.

Object of the game: to have fun.

How to play: the children join hands in a circle. The leader (teacher or assistant) walks or skips the children around the circle singing:

Ring around the rosy
A pocket full of posies
Ash-a! Ash-a!
We all fall down.

On the word "down" everyone collapses to the ground.

For a bit more fun you could change the last line of the song to "We all kneel down" or "We all jump high" and so on.

3
DAY-CARE LICENSING

This chapter is where you begin to understand what day care is all about. It will not be enough for you to hang out your shingle, take in as many children as possible, and hope all goes well.

In every state and province in North America, there is what Barbara Willer in the book *Caring for Children, Challenge to America*, calls "a baseline or floor of quality below which no service may legally operate." Through a combination of licensing regulations, zoning restrictions, health standards, and building and safety codes, governments see to it that children of all age levels receive a minimum standard of care.

By wielding sanctions varying from conditions placed against a license to the closure of a facility, the regulatory government offices have the power to ensure the basic standards are met.

In exchange for your promise to meet and uphold the minimal standards set by your local, state, or provincial government for operating a day care, you will be given a license to operate. Before a license will be issued, you must demonstrate compliance with rules relating to adult/child ratios, caregiver or staff qualifications, quality programming, proper physical environment, and health, safety, and administration. Through the regulation of these procedures, the government ensures parents their children will be provided with safe and quality child care. A list of state and provincial licensing offices is located in Appendix 1.

Licensing requirements in both Canada and the United States have come a long way in the last 25 years, mostly as a result of reports like the National Day Care Study (NDCS), conducted in the United States. The study focused on how the development of preschool children is affected by —

(a) child/staff ratio,

(b) group size,

(c) caregiver qualifications, and

(d) other programming components which can be regulated.

As a result of these findings, the NDCS was able to formulate a basic bottom line for care that could be adopted by governments. The NDCS research found that small groups, supervised by caregivers with training in child development or early childhood education worked best because the caregiver was able to be actively involved with children in these groups.

Through the NDCS findings and the Comparative Licensing Study conducted in the United States by the Administration for Children, Youth, and Families (ACYF), governments set standards for all categories of child care. Although these standards vary considerably from region to region, they focus on child/staff ratios, group size, caregiver qualifications, program outlines, physical environment, health and safety precautions, nutrition, parental involvement, and administration. Let's take a close look at these components.

a. GROUP SIZE

The restrictions put on the number of children allowed in a family day care vary with each state and province. For instance, Montana allows a maximum of six children in a home day care, with no more than three children under the age of two, including the caregiver's own. Saskatchewan allows not more than eight children, provided only five are in the preschool, toddler, or infant group and no more than two children are infants.

Six seems to be a common maximum group size; some areas allow eight if two are school-age and no more than three children are under two. Read your licensing requirements thoroughly and if these regulations are unclear, question them.

b. CAREGIVER QUALIFICATIONS

What does it take to become a child-care provider? Many people would contend that, unlike other professions, anyone can look after children. This could not be further from the truth.

To be successful in this field, you need to think of yourself as a professional; you are someone who is dedicated to the children in your care and their families. You are also dedicated to being the best care provider you can be. You must have the desire to improve your skills.

Individual governments have their own standards for caregiver qualifications. The type of training needed to satisfy the basic licensing requirements can be as strict as Alberta's, which state that all new day-care centers must "Employ directors who have obtained advanced-level certification," and "One in four day care workers must possess training in childhood development or early childhood education, equivalent to a one-year certificate," or as lax as the states that barely make child development or early childhood education a prerequisite to setting up a facility.

Many states have adopted regulations requiring one staff member per center to possess a Child Development Associate Credential. Others require caregivers to have bachelor's degrees in early childhood education or child development.

Regulations differ, but there are requirements that are standard in the industry. The minimum criteria for a day-care provider are the following:

- You must be 18 years of age or older.

- You must have two references (written statements).

- You must have a physician's letter stating your mental and physical ability to perform this type of work.

- You must be willing to sign a release form allowing a local police reference check or investigation authorization which looks into criminal records and child abuse registries on you and each adult member of your household.

- You must have a current first aid or CPR certificate.

- Your house and equipment must pass health, fire, and sanitation inspections.

- You must be willing to take 20 hours of in-service training in early childhood education, child development, or related courses per year.

c. PROGRAM OUTLINES

The Saskatchewan Child Care Act, Section 27, Part III, Standards For Facilities, states that —

> Every licensee shall establish:
>
> (a) a statement of the philosophy and goals of the facility;
>
> (b) policies with respect to the operation of the facility;
>
> and shall make these known to the parents of the children attending the facility.

Every licensee shall establish a daily program plan and, without limiting the generality of the foregoing, each daily program plan shall make adequate provision for an environment that is developmentally appropriate for:

(a) the children of the ages of those attending the facility and,

(b) each child

and shall make the daily program known to parents of the children attending the facility.

Programming, like group size and staff/child ratio, plays an important role in maintaining a minimum standard of care for all children. Studying the program outlines of various, well-established centers will help you develop a program that will enhance child development through a variety of stimulating activities and quiet times, while at the same time establishing the consistency of daily routines that will help children develop a sense of trust and security.

For more on developing your program, see chapter 10.

d. PHYSICAL ENVIRONMENT

Children flourish in surroundings that are brightly lit, colorfully decorated, and well stocked with books, toys, and age-appropriate equipment such as child-size chairs and tables, and where there is an abundance of indoor and outdoor space to crawl around or run in.

In fact, some licensing boards actually set out the size of a room for a certain number of children or limit the amount of unobstructed indoor space for each child. For example, the requirements for the Registration of a Family Day Care Home in Montana stipulate that —

11.14.403, Family Day Care Homes, Building Requirements,
1) All areas used for day care purposes must have at least one door for egress of not less than 34" wide and a minimum of one other means of

egress at least 24" high by 20" wide of full clear opening. All exits must be obstructed at all times.

In addition to these requirements, you can add a host of other rules and regulations governing everything from well-ventilated basements to closet doors that can be opened from the inside, to premises that are free of insects, rodents, and other vermin.

Children need an environment that's safe and properly equipped. There should be a crib or a playpen for each infant and enough high chairs and infant seats with safety straps. Adequate diaper-changing areas and toilet-training areas are also part of a well-designed physical environment.

Your day care will also need an outdoor play space and outdoor equipment. Any outdoor play supplies should be age appropriate and in sufficient supply to support the number of children using them.

A general rule of thumb, you should read your licensing requirements thoroughly to make sure your home meets the standards set by the licensing board. Regulations for minimum standards may seem obvious, but they are there to protect the children.

e. HEALTH AND SAFETY

The health aspect of licensing for child care encompasses everything from basic hygiene to administering medication.

For example, in Alabama, the Minimum Standards for Day Care Centers and Night Time Centers require the following:

(a) Medical information which must be on file: results of medical examinations, screening, or assessment; record of immunization and lists (if indicated)

(b) Illness and injury: inspections, isolation and removal, communicable diseases, re-admission, first aid, emergency plan, authority and procedure for administering medicine

(c) Hygienic practices: face and hand washing, toilet articles, extra children's clothing, presence of healthy animals who pose no threat

Safety, on the other hand, pertains to the prevention of injuries and accidents. Government licensing standards relating to safety focus basically on —

(a) the secure storage of poisonous substances,

(b) security caps on all electrical outlets accessible to children,

(c) approved first aid kits,

(d) safety equipment such as fire extinguishers and smoke detectors,

(e) staff training in child CPR and first aid, and

(f) the establishment of procedures to be followed for medical and fire emergencies.

Check the regulations for your state or province carefully. For example, provincial regulations in Newfoundland deal with day-care safety standards for everything from barbecuing outside to natural Christmas trees.

f. NUTRITION

"What's in a meal?" you might ask. "Plenty," would be a good answer if one looks at how nutrition for day care is regarded under the law. According to the booklet *Minimum Standards for Nutritional Care in Child Care Facilities* published by the Department of Health for Mississippi, "Nutrition and feeding is an important part of day-care services for young children. No single period is as critical for nutritional well-being throughout the life cycle as the years from conception to age six."

Like Section 27 of the Saskatchewan Child Care Act, that requires food to be served "within three hours of the facility opening each day" and that not more than three hours should elapse between meals and or snacks, Mississippi also regulates "food needs based on length of time spent in child care facility."

Most other states and provinces have similar guidelines for nutrition, including mealtime schedules and eating places, menus, special diets, food preparation, and infant feedings. While regulations do not specify exactly what foods must be fed to children, they do base their daily requirements on the U.S. Department of Agriculture's Nutrition Pyramid or in Canada, the Canada Food Guide issued by Health and Welfare Canada. For example, the Northwest Territories' Child Day Care Act states that where a meal is provided, it is recommended by nutritionists that it be balanced and follow the Canada Food Guide of at least —

- one serving of milk and milk products,

- one serving of meat or meat alternatives, and

- two servings of fruit and vegetables.

Where a snack is provided, it is recommended that it consist of at least —

- one serving of bread and cereals,

- one serving of fruit and vegetables, and

- either one serving of milk and milk products or one serving of meat and meat alternatives.

g. PARENTAL INVOLVEMENT

Parents are an integral part of any child care program. It is imperative you establish at the onset a working relationship with each parent who uses your services. To ensure that communication with parents is fostered, some licensing authorities require the formation of a parent advisory council.

h. ADMINISTRATION (OPERATING PROCEDURES)

Behind every successful business is a well-managed administration. This is the who, what, where, and how of operating procedures.

- Who will handle what activities?

- Who will insure your business, do maintenance, and repairs?

- Who will take over in case of emergency?

- What are your hours, house rules, fees, policies, procedures, menus, objectives, and child activities?

- Where will you operate, get additional funding, find staff, and get your ideas for constructive activities?

- How will you make your policies known to the parents of the children attending your center and how will you ensure employees and parents comply with these procedures?

And most of all, how will all this fit together into one neat little package called day care?

You will need to give all of this considerable thought because just as surely as you are asking yourself these questions now, the licensing office in your location will be doing the same.

i. GETTING YOUR LICENSE

Outlined below are the procedures for getting your license to operate a family day care from your home. Check your state or provincial guidelines; the procedures and paperwork required may vary .

(a) Go to your municipal and/or state/provincial office and obtain the applications necessary to start a home day care. If you don't know whom to contact, inquire at any day care center.

(b) Review the application thoroughly to make certain you understand exactly what is required to meet the standards for space, equipment, staff qualifications, and child/staff ratios as we reviewed.

(c) With regulations in hand, go carefully through your house room by room and note any changes you will have to make to conform to regulations.

(d) Contact authorities with regard to zoning. Make appointments with the inspection unit of your local health department. Call your local fire department for a fire inspection. Get all the necessary papers to be handed in with your application.

(e) Set up an appointment with a day-care coordinator to visit your home and discuss the licensing procedures.

(f) Make your plans for qualifying. If you need to do some home renovations, estimate costs and time required. Get estimates and delivery time on needed equipment. Take any required courses (e.g., first aid, early childhood education).

(g) Get written references and a physician's note. Complete the required police reference check or investigation authorization.

(h) Arrange for final inspection.

(i) When all requirements are fulfilled, complete and submit your application for licensing. Include all necessary papers.

(j) Receive your license.

Getting a license for your home day care may seem like a farfetched dream at this point, but rest assured that you can do it. To give yourself confidence, visit and talk with the operators or directors of quality day cares. Pick their brains, ask for their help, even volunteer a few hours a week at the day care you most admire and learn, first hand, how they operate. That way you will see that you can do it, too!

j. UNLICENSED DAY CARE

Should you go to all the trouble of getting your license, since many people provide care without one? Only you can decide. In most states and provinces it is illegal to take money for providing child care without first being licensed. However, we all know there are no day-care police scouring unsuspecting neighborhoods for unlicensed facilities.

People who choose not to be licensed do so for these reasons —

- They want to avoid income tax,

- They want to avoid being subject to inspections, and

- They only want to look after one or two children.

Getting licensed is worth doing not only because it's the law, but for other very important reasons:

- Parents would rather send their child to a licensed facility when given the choice. They feel more at ease knowing their child is receiving monitored care and that the provider is, at minimum, meeting government standards.

- Insurance companies may refuse coverage if you are not licensed. If anything goes wrong or a child is hurt, you could be sued. Without insurance you have no protection whatsoever.

- Business deductions associated with your licensed facility often offset any taxes you may incur.

- You may not be able to register with a referral agency unless you are licensed.

- In the United States, you can only claim a food expense reimbursement with the Childcare Food Program if you are licensed.

In all honesty, it is not that difficult to get your license. True, you may have to make a few improvements to your home, or purchase equipment, but if you plan to provide day care for any length of time and you want your business to be profitable, it is well worth your while to get licensed. Don't forget: renovations and other purchases can only be deducted when you are licensed.

Peanut Butter & Honey Balls

⅔ cup chunky peanut butter

⅓ cup honey

1 cup nonfat dry milk

raisins, sesame seeds,

Rice Krispies (optional)

- Blend peanut butter and honey in a bowl.
- Gradually work in milk and raisins, sesame seeds, or Rice Krispies with hands.
- Shape into balls.
- Chill.
- Store covered in the refrigerator.

4

SETTING UP SHOP

Although you may prefer to think of yourself as a child-care provider rather than as a small business owner, you must begin running your day care as a business or you will find yourself in deep water very soon. This chapter talks about a few of the business matters you will need to attend to before opening your doors.

a. LEGAL ADVICE

1. Finding a lawyer

If you do not already have a lawyer, you should contact your local lawyer referral service. The referral service will refer you to a lawyer who takes on small business clients like you. Through this system you will be eligible for a 30-minute consultation for a nominal fee, after which you and the lawyer can establish a fee arrangement. Ask the lawyer up front what his or her fees are and how they are calculated. Don't be shy about doing this. Your new venture is going to take a considerable amount of capital, and you'll need to include your legal fees into your start-up costs. It may even pay you to shop around if you believe the lawyer's fees are too high.

2. Your first meeting

During your initial consultation, you should discuss the following:

(a) How will you be charged: an hourly rate, fixed rate, percentage fee, or lump sum fee?

(b) What will the exact fee or percentage be?

(c) What the total cost of disbursements and fees will be or if you can get an estimate?

(d) Will the lawyer require a retainer and if so, how much, or will you pay when your case is completed?

Whatever you agree on, *get it in writing.*

3. Keeping legal costs down

To help you keep your legal costs to a minimum, you have to understand that you are purchasing your lawyer's time; therefore, the less time you use, the less you pay. Here are a few tips to help you keep these costs down:

(a) Have all necessary papers and documents together and in order before visiting your lawyer.

(b) Have a list of issues you need advice on.

(c) Give the lawyer as much information as possible

(d) Ask what you can do to assist with your case and reduce your costs.

(e) Resist making unnecessary phone calls. Write to your lawyer instead unless you need an immediate answer.

4. The Child Care Law Center

The Child Care Law Center is an organization in the United States that works exclusively on the legal issues concerning the establishment and provision of child care. The center's objective is to use legal tools to promote the creation of quality, affordable child care. It provides legal services and assistance to lawyers, child-care providers, parents, and others concerned about developing quality child-care programs.

Through a variety of programs and publications, the Child Care Law Center offers you and your lawyer expert advice on licensing regulations and enforcement practices, variances with regards to zoning, building codes, covenants in homeowners' agreements, and so on. If you are having any difficulties in these areas or you simply want more information on their services, you or your lawyer can contact them at the Child Care Law Center, 22 Second Street, San Francisco, California 84105, (415) 495-5498.

b. NAMING YOUR BUSINESS

Picture yourself as a kid for a few minutes. Go ahead! Close your eyes, take a deep breath and release all your stress and anxieties. Now, visualize this big, bright, fun-to-be-in day care. There are other kids around and great toys to play with. If you were a kid, which you are for the moment, what would you call this wonderland? What would that neat sign on the front lawn say about this great place? What is the best thing you remember about your childhood or your first weeks in kindergarten when everything was new and exciting? Take your time and think, really hard. What should you name your day care?

Naming your day care is a very important step in setting up for business. It reflects what you do, what type of business you run. Your name should spell out *Welcome* to all who pass through your doors. Your day care will be where children will go every day for many days of their lives. It will be their home, their playground, and their school. Choosing a name, therefore, should be done carefully.

First, write down every name you can think of. Then narrow your selection down

to three favorites, placing the name you like best at the top.

There is a reason for choosing three names. Before you apply to register your business, for your own protection and to avoid potential legal conflicts, you should make certain no other day care is using the same name. Technically, this is called a name search. You can do a name search yourself by scouting your local Yellow Pages, newspaper classified ads, trade journals, and special-interest publications geared for the day-care market. While doing your search, check out all three names you have in mind. That way, if your first choice doesn't pan out, you will already know if your second choice is available. Before you invest in stationery, advertising, and a sign, you want to be absolutely sure that you can, legally, use the name.

A name search in Canada can also be done through the provincial ministry responsible for corporate affairs. For a nominal fee and a wait of about a week, you will have government assurance that the name you selected can form the legal identity of your day care. In the United States, county or city clerks can do a name search for you.

Once you have your day care name approved, you'll need to file your business name, also known as a DBA (doing business as) or statement of fictitious business name, with your local, state, or provincial government. In some cases you may also be required to publish your intent to use the name in your local newspaper.

If you intend to use your personal name as your business name, for example, Jane Smith's Day Care, you are not required to file your registration. It is however, advisable to do so for your own protection.

c. YOUR BUSINESS STRUCTURE

The day care operator, like any good business person, should choose the business structure most suitable for his or her enterprise. The question is, do you wish to function as a sole proprietorship, partnership, or corporation?

1. Sole proprietorship

Sole proprietorship is the structure most often used by people setting up a home day care. It is the simplest and least expensive way to start out. As the sole proprietor, you alone control the business. This means that any profits or losses incurred with your business are included as part of your personal income. This type of structure allows you flexibility in transferring funds between your business and personal accounts. Many businesses start as sole proprietorships and incorporate later.

2. Partnership

When you join together with another person or other persons to form your business, you are essentially establishing a partnership. A partnership may take various forms. For example, you might go into an agreement with someone who is your financial backer, yet wants nothing to do with the actual running of the day care. On the other hand, the partnership could be an agreement between two people who will share both expenses or losses and the work load.

You should have your lawyer draw up an agreement that specifies —

(a) how the partnership is to be run,

(b) how the earnings and losses are to be split,

(c) dissolution proceedings, and

(d) a mediation clause to solve disputes.

Since you and your partner(s) are responsible for any debts and obligations of the partnership as a whole, it is best to go into business with someone you can trust.

3. Incorporation

When you form an incorporated company, you create a separate and distinct entity. The business will have a life of its own. It will, from that point on, have its own identity separate and apart from you and your partners, if any. You will no longer be personally responsible for any debts or any suits filed against your business. With incorporation, you can sell shares to help fund your day care.

You will, however, be subject to more regulations from state/provincial and federal authorities and you will be responsible for filing separate tax returns for the corporation to the state/provincial and federal governments.

The process of incorporation can be a lengthy and costly one. It is possible in some states or provinces to do your own incorporation rather than paying a lawyer to do it for you. Self-Counsel Press publishes incorporation guides for several states and provinces; see the back of this book for more information.

Note: The limited liability aspect of incorporated companies is often of little value to the start-up business person as most professional lenders will require a personal guarantee when you borrow money.

As you can see, there are pros and cons to each structure. In making your decision, consider taxation levels, regulations, and commercial law as it affects your business. Professional advice from an accountant and lawyer will prove helpful in your decision-making process. Remember, it is possible to start your business as a proprietorship and incorporate it later when the business warrants it.

d. INSURANCE

Running a day care without having some form of liability insurance is much like playing Russian roulette. You never really know from one day to the next when a child might get hurt or severely injured while in your care, but you take for granted that because you are so safety-conscious, it could never happen. Until one day it does. The child's parents have no medical insurance and are suing you for negligence and for the cost of the child's medical care. You stand to loose your business, your house, and everything else you have worked your whole life for. A scary prospect.

Liability insurance is purchased as a security blanket. It covers you against suits of negligence or failure to exercise reasonable care that result from accidents having occurred to a child while in your care or on your premises. Liability insurance is available in two distinctly different packages.

General liability insurance usually covers bodily injury, property damage, medical costs for treatment at the time of the incident, and legal defense in the event a suit is filed against you for neglect or any other reason except abuse. (Most insurance companies exclude physical and sexual abuse from their general liability packages.)

Comprehensive general liability insurance covers incidents that happen both on the day-care premises and away from the program site. This type of coverage may be purchased separately for such things as personal injury, transportation insurance, owner's and tenant's liability, fire legal liability, and professional liability, to name a few.

Both these liability packages can be purchased as one of two types: *claims made* and *occurrence*. A claims made policy only covers you for claims made during the time your policy is in effect. With an occurrence policy, you are protected from claims as a result of an accident or injury that happened while the policy was in effect. For example, little Trevor slips and breaks his leg while playing outside in your yard in December. Your current insurance policy runs out on December 31. In January, the parents decide to sue. Under an occurrence policy, you would still be covered because

the accident occurred while the policy was in effect. Under a claims made policy, you would not be covered, because the claim was not made while the policy was in effect.

Designing a liability package for your day care takes an understanding of what a policy includes or excludes. In some cases, the things a company will not insure you for take up more space on the policy form than the actual coverage itself. It is important to question your insurer about the many aspects of your policy. Moreover, if the policy does not cover your basic needs or what you consider to be the essentials, shop elsewhere.

Finding liability insurance to protect all your needs may not be easy. To find out more about your particular insurance needs and where you can locate a reputable insurance company that handles these requirements, talk to —

(a) your personal insurance agent. If he or she cannot help or offer you a quality package, ask if he or she can refer you to someone who handles day-care insurance.

(b) other care providers in your area. Find out who covers them and what their insurance package entails.

(c) your local licensing board. They may know insurance companies that provide what you are looking for.

(d) local and national child-care organizations. Again, they may be able to refer you to an insurance company.

The Child Care Action Campaign (CCAC) has a book titled *Insuring your Future: Liability Insurance and Child Care* that offers information about designing a liability package. The book also profiles 25 insurance companies from various parts of the United States that offer liability insurance. The book can be ordered directly from CCAC. They also publish an information guide titled *Child Care Liability Insurance*.

The Child Care Law Center also has a great many publications available to the public that deal with insurance and tax issues. You can receive a publications list by writing to them (see address in Appendix 2).

Some other insurance you may need to purchase include —

(a) motor vehicle insurance

(b) accident insurance, and

(c) worker's compensation.

It is very likely that you will be transporting the children to and from prearranged outings or school. Therefore, your motor vehicle insurance should be reviewed or changed to ensure that you have sufficient insurance to protect you in the event of an accident.

The extra protection from accident insurance may be a good investment, as it can help cover medical costs of an injured child.

If you hire any staff, you will be required in many states and provinces to purchase worker's compensation.

Realizing that you need insurance is one thing, but finding a company who will offer you the protection you need at a price you can afford is another. That, in a nutshell, is the hard news about insurance and the day-care industry. Some insurance companies have been known to refuse liability insurance to providers; others put limits on the number of children they will insure. You will need to discuss your situation with your agent or broker. Ask about the possibility of adding a rider onto your current homeowner or tenant's policy to include the extra coverage. Whatever arrangements you make, have whoever is handling your policy formalize your coverage by putting it in writing.

e. YOUR PROJECT LOG

You may find your activities for setting up shop a lot less hectic if you use a project log similar to the one shown in Worksheet #4.

WORKSHEET #4
PROJECT LOG

ACTIVITY	DATE STARTED	DATE COMPLETED
CALLS TO:		
Resource and referral agency		
Social service office		
Elementary school		
Parent advisory council		
Personnel departments of local businesses		
Child care facility #1		
Child care facility #2		
Child care facility #3		
Regional planning committee		
CHILD-CARE NEED ASSESSMENT		
Phone interviews		
In-person interviews		
Mail-out questionnaire		
Questionnaire budgeting		
Questionnaire analysis		
LICENSING		
Pick up application		
Study application		
Medical examination		
Tuberculin test		
Physician's recommendation		
Four references		
Application filed		

WORKSHEET #4 — Continued

ACTIVITY	DATE STARTED	DATE COMPLETED
BUILDING INSPECTION Fire marshal Health inspector Sanitation officer Obtain written reports		
LEGAL ADVICE Lawyer referral service Initial consultation Fees discussed		
ZONING Get details from city hall Review Pass onto lawyer for review Apply for variances if necessary		
CONTACT CONTRACTORS Quotes on renovations		
NAME YOUR DAY CARE OR DAY HOME Search local sources Have name search done Complete and send in application		
BUSINESS STRUCTURE Discuss with lawyer Discuss with accountant File appropriate papers		

ACTIVITY	DATE STARTED	DATE COMPLETED
GRANTS AND FUNDS Contact local state/ provincial social services Put in applications		
SEND FOR INFORMATION FROM Child care law center Equipment and toy suppliers		
OTHER		

The Farmer in the Dell

This is best played in a larger group.

Object of the game: the best objective there is — to enjoy yourself.

How to play: one child is the Farmer and stands inside the circle. The rest of the children join hands and walk or skip around the Farmer, singing the song. For the second verse the Farmer chooses someone from the circle to be the Wife. The Farmer rejoins the others and the Wife then stands in the circle, and so on:

> The Farmer in the dell,
> The Farmer in the dell,
> Hi Ho the derry-o,
> The Farmer in the dell.
>
> The Farmer takes a Wife,
> The Farmer takes a Wife,
> Hi Ho the derry-o,
> The Farmer takes a Wife.
>
> The Wife takes a Child,
> The Wife takes a Child,
> Hi Ho the derry-o,
> The Wife takes a Child.
>
> The Child takes a Dog...
> The Dog takes a Cat...
> The Cat takes a Rat...
> The Rat takes the Cheese...
> The Cheese stands alone...

At this point everyone circles around the Cheese singing:

> The Cheese stands alone,
> The Cheese stands alone,
> Hi Ho the derry-o,
> The Cheese stands alone.

The unfavored Cheese then becomes the Farmer in the next round.

5

MONEY MATTERS:
YOUR START-UP AND OPERATING BUDGETS

There's no doubt about it — starting and running your day-care business is going to require money, at least at first. To find out how much, you are going to have to estimate your expenses and do both a start-up budget and an estimated operating budget.

a. YOUR START-UP COSTS

Before you can even open your doors, you will be spending money on —

(a) renovations,

(b) toys and equipment,

(c) furnishings,

(d) office supplies,

(e) telephone installation,

(f) insurance premiums,

(g) legal, accounting, and licensing fees,

(h) advertising and promotion expenses,

(i) creating your business structure,

(j) food, and

(k) bank charges (setting up accounts).

In addition, you should have set aside a generous sum allotted to operating expenses until your day care reaches capacity and is fully operational.

The actual amount of costs will, of course, depend on how elaborate you make your facility. One way to approach start-up budgeting is to work out two budgets, one that is absolutely bare-bones, with everything done at minimum cost and only the essentials provided, and the other an extravagant wish list with everything done just right and all the trimmings in place. From looking at these two budgets, you can decide where your budget will fall. If you've got the money to go "all out," great. Just remember this is a business you are running and don't get too caught up in a buying frenzy. If you find that even the minimum budget is beyond your means, you're obviously going to have to rethink your plan and possibly look for money sources.

More likely, you will find that you can afford more than the bare bones, but not quite so much as the maximum budget. You can then decide where you want to compromise and where you want to spend any extra money.

While many of your start-up costs are more or less fixed, the amounts you allot to toys, furnishings, and equipment, particularly, will be subject to variation, so you will probably spend a good deal of your budgeting time on pricing and budgeting for these items.

I hope by now you have established a good rapport with a few day-care providers, because the best place to start your budgeting is in their facilities. Take a look at what they use and ask what brands they prefer. If an item looks well-used but still in good shape, take that as a sign. Ask where these caregivers purchased their equipment and toys, then contact the suppliers and request catalogs and pricing information. Find out what their delivery time is so you can make sure your orders are placed in time to receive and set up everything before your opening day.

The following is a list of some of the items you'll need to set up for child care. The need for many of the items will depend on the ages of the children you will be caring for.

- high chairs
- infant seats
- booster chairs
- small tables and chairs
- cribs
- cots
- blankets
- sheets
- pillows
- diaper-changing tables
- diaper pails
- storage shelves
- outdoor adventure centers
- sand box
- swings
- solid surfaces for tricycles and doll buggies
- indoor water and sand tables
- plastic containers to store small toys
- toss cushions or bean bags for floor play
- toys
- musical equipment such as records, tapes, and record players
- books
- art and craft supplies

Outfitting your day care with all this equipment will take a considerable amount of your start-up capital. To stay within budget, first make a list of everything you would like to have for your facility using the first page of Worksheet #5. Then order your list by priority, putting numbers next to each item according to how important it is. For example, if you are going to look after infants, changing tables and diapers pails are going to be a necessity, not a luxury, so they would be item 1 or 2 on your list.

When you've set your priorities, list everything again using the second page of Worksheet #5, this time putting the high priority items at the top and low priority items at the bottom. Using your catalogs and other research, price everything in your list. Now, you can start adding things up from the top to see what will fit in your budget. If you add up the first five items and you've already overstepped your budget, you will probably need to adjust your figures.

At this point, you may have to start making choices and compromises. For example, you may have to choose between an adventure playground and a swing set, as both are expensive items.

It may be worth noting here that not all the equipment and toys you purchase have to be new or ordered from a catalog. Garage sales and flea markets are excellent sources of used supplies. With a good cleaning and a thorough inspection for broken or loose parts, and perhaps a bit of lead-free paint, your used equipment will be as good as new. Buying used equipment can help you fit more into your budget.

Health and Welfare Canada publishes a booklet called *Facilities and Equipment for Day Care Centres*, which is full of ideas on designing layouts and choosing equipment and supplies. You can obtain a copy by writing to the National Child Care Information Centre, Social Service Programs Branch, Ottawa, Ontario, Canada K1A 1B5.

Now, complete Worksheet #6 to help you establish a start-up budget.

WORKSHEET #5
PRICING START-UP EQUIPMENT

ITEM	PRIORITY

PRIORITY	ITEM	PRICE ESTIMATE
1. _____		_____
2. _____		_____
3. _____		_____
4. _____		_____
5. _____		_____
6. _____		_____
7. _____		_____
8. _____		_____
9. _____		_____
10. _____		_____
11. _____		_____
12. _____		_____
13. _____		_____
14. _____		_____
15. _____		_____
16. _____		_____
17. _____		_____
18. _____		_____
19. _____		_____
20. _____		_____
21. _____		_____
22. _____		_____
23. _____		_____
24. _____		_____
25. _____		_____
26. _____		_____

WORKSHEET #6
START-UP BUDGET

	Maximum budget	Minimum budget	Your budget
Renovations			
Toys			
Equipment			
Furnishings			
Office supplies			
Telephone installation			
Insurance premiums			
Legal fees			
Accounting fees			
Licensing fees			
Advertising and promotion expenses			
Creating your business structure			
Food			
Bank charges			
Operating expenses fund			
TOTAL			

b. YOU NEED MONEY — WHERE CAN YOU GO?

The figures you arrive at when you work out your start-up costs represent in plain dollar signs your expected initial outlay of cash. These figures are important for a few reasons:

(a) They allow you to arrange for additional financing or rearrange your budget if you know you will fall short.

(b) They give financial backers a clear picture of how their money will be used.

(c) Forecasting, start-up or otherwise, is a healthy business practice.

If you discover that you need additional cash to start your day care, you have several possibilities for finding financing:

(a) Relatives and friends

(b) Banks and other lending institutions

(c) Government

1. Relatives and friends

"Love money" refers to money loaned on the basis of personal relationships — family ties, love, or friendship. This kind of loan can be a wonderful gift of affection, but it can also cause major rifts. If the business is successful and the money is repaid promptly, both parties remain happy and satisfied. There are good feelings all around. If the business falters, on the other hand, and the loan is not repaid, the borrowed money can become a contentious issue that survives much longer than the ill-fated enterprise.

Before taking "love money," consider carefully how you will pay the money back if your business fails and whether the loan is worth a possible conflict with your relative or friend. Make the transaction as businesslike as possible and be scrupulous in honoring the trust that is inherent in such a loan. Prepare a proper promissory note

that outlines the terms and conditions. Promissory notes can be purchased at many stationery stores.

2. Banks and other lending institutions

If you choose to use a bank or other lending institution for your financing, it is important that you present as business-like an image as possible. You want to be treated as a business, so you have to act like a business. You will have to prepare a simple business plan and be ready to answer all the banker's questions about your business's projected costs, income, etc. (For more information on business plans, see *Preparing a Successful Business Plan*, another title in the Self-Counsel Series.) You will also have to show that you are committed to your business by demonstrating that you will invest your own finances and that you have done some research and analysis into your business prospects.

All this can be intimidating for a first-time business operator but it is no more than the bank will expect. One alternative would be to simply borrow the money you need as a personal loan. You will not need a business plan, nor will you need to explain the details of your business. If the amount you need is small and you have the collateral to back up the loan, this may be the easiest choice.

3. Government

Most states and provinces, through government departments dealing with social services, operate some form of assistance programs for day cares. These programs can range from grants for start-up, emergency repair or relocation, to operating allowances which assist with the everyday costs of providing day-care services. For more information on available funding in your area, contact your local social services office.

c. YOUR OPERATING BUDGET

The money comes in (parent fees), the money goes out (toys, food), and whatever is left is profit. Sounds simple enough. And it is — if you organize your income and expense files in a civilized manner and cross your heart you'll maintain that filing system if it kills you.

One of your first priorities in establishing an easy-to-follow record-keeping system is to work out an operating budget. The operating budget systematically lays out your estimated income and expenses for each month. It will establish categories so you can maintain ongoing income/expense records; give it some careful thought.

d. ESTIMATING INCOME

Your major source of income will be, of course, the fees paid by the parents. To estimate your income from this source each month, you will simply multiply the number of children in each fee category by the fee for that category, then add up the totals. For example, if you take in one infant, two toddlers, and two school-age children, your income calculation would be:

1 infant	@ $400	= 400
2 toddlers	@ $300	= 600
2 school-age	@ $250	= 500
TOTAL		1,500

In some places, the government may offer day-care subsidies or other grants. You would then add the subsidy payments into your income.

Your income estimate should be based on the assumption that you will fill all available spaces every month. Under most circumstances, you should have no difficulty achieving this. The demand for day care is such that with little marketing or advertising, you will probably have a waiting list in many cases.

e. ESTIMATING EXPENSES

To estimate your expenses, you will need to work out rough budgets for everything you will be using. In all the costing done below, we will assume that you have decided how many children you will be taking in and that you will always have that many children coming in.

1. Food costs

For example, to determine what your food costs will be, work out a couple of weekly menu plans, then cost them out. Worksheet #7 and Sample #3 will help you do some food costing.

First, enter which meal you are costing out — lunch, morning snack, afternoon snack, etc.

For each food item, decide on the most efficient size to purchase. Mark down the product, purchase size (e.g., 454 grams, 1 dozen, etc.), and price.

Establish how many servings a package contains. A serving might be one egg, one slice of bread, or a half cup of cereal. Divide the purchase price by the number of servings in the package and you have the cost per serving. Then, total your serving costs and you have a cost per meal. Total your meal costs and you have a cost per child per day. This figure multiplied by 20 working days in a month gives you the monthly food costs per child. Add up the monthly food costs for all the children and you have your total food costs for the month.

2. Supply costs

Besides food, there are many other supplies you will need. Don't discount these as insignificant; a small cheap item that is used on a regular basis can quickly add up. For example, three children can use a lot of toilet paper. Each item may only be a dollar or so per week, but when you consider the dozens of items you will be providing on a daily basis, your expenses could easily add up to many dollars every week.

WORKSHEET #7
FOOD COST ANALYSIS

Meal_____

Item	Size	Price	# of servings	Cost per serving

Total cost per meal [____]

Meal_____

Item	Size	Price	# of servings	Cost per serving

Total cost per meal [____]

Meal_____

Item	Size	Price	# of servings	Cost per serving

Total cost per meal [____]

Cost per meal 1 ___ + cost per meal 2 ___ + cost per meal 3 ___
= Food cost per child per day

Food cost per day x 20 = Food cost per child per month

SAMPLE #3
FOOD COST ANALYSIS

Meal___Breakfast___

Item	Size	Price	# of servings	Cost per serving
Juice	1 litre	$1.20	4	30¢
Toast	450 g	$1.99	24	8¢
Apple	900g	$1.80	6	30¢

Total cost per meal ___68¢___

Meal___Snack___

Item	Size	Price	# of servings	Cost per serving
Carrot	900g	80¢	10	8¢
Crackers	450 g	$2.49	25	10¢
Cheese	227g	$2.76	7	39¢

Total cost per meal ___57¢___

Meal___Lunch___

Item	Size	Price	# of servings	Cost per serving
Weiners	900g	$2.50	12	21¢
Bun	450g	$2.50	12	21¢
Fruit cups	900g	$3.56	4	89¢
Juice	1 litre	$1.20	4	30¢

Total cost per meal ___$1.61___

Cost per meal 1 ___ + cost per meal 2 ___ + cost per meal 3 ___
= Food cost per child per day

Food cost per day x 20 = Food cost per child per month

45

Here are a few of the non-food supplies you will be using regularly:

- disinfectant
- dish soap
- laundry soap (for towels and face cloths)
- hand soap
- toilet paper
- tissues
- toothpaste
- paper towels
- construction paper
- glue
- paper
- coloring books
- crayons
- felt pens
- pencils
- chalk
- paint

Remember to include the cost of gas for your car if you intend to do regular field trips or will be expected to pick up children from school.

Use Worksheet #8 to list some of the supplies you anticipate using and their costs. Sample #4 shows Worksheet #8 completed for a fictional day care.

List the item in the first column (toothpaste, disinfectant). Then list the size of the item (100 grams, 6 rolls) and the price. Now, you need to estimate the number of "uses" you (or the children) will get out of that item. You might guess that you get 50 squirts of disinfectant out of a bottle or 30 squeezes of toothpaste out of a tube. Divide the price by the number of "uses" and you have the price per "use." Your next task is to estimate how many times in the week you will use that item. For example, if you are looking after two infants who each need their diaper changed 4 times per day, and you use the disinfectant each time to clean up the diaper-changing area, you are looking at 2 infants x 4 changes per day x 5 days per week = 40 "uses" of disinfectant per week. Finally, multiply the "uses" per week by the price per "use" and you have the cost per week. Add up the weekly costs for all supplies, and you have a total supply cost per week. This figure multiplied by four weeks in a month gives you the total supply cost for the month.

Remember, this cost is the total for all children in your day care. To get the cost per child (as when estimating expenses for setting rates), you will need to divide the total cost per month by the number of children.

3. Equipment replacement costs

Then there are the items that don't get "used up," but which do eventually wear out, get broken, or get lost:

- toys
- towels
- face cloths
- toothbrushes
- scissors
- paint brushes
- chairs
- easels
- games

Don't forget any special food equipment you might be using frequently for the children. For example, if you are going to give them freshly squeezed juice every day and you use an electric juicer, that juicer is going to wear out some day. Replacing it is a real cost of running your day care.

TOTAL SUPPLY COST PER WEEK

Item	Size	Price	# of uses in item	Cost per use	# of uses per week	Cost per week

Total supply cost per week _____

Total supply cost per week x 4 = Total supply cost per month

Total supply cost per month ÷ number of children in day care = supply cost per child per month

TOTAL SUPPLY COST PER WEEK

Item	Size	Price	# of uses in item	Cost per use	# of uses per week	Cost per week
Liquid Soap	600 mL	$3.00	65	.05¢	15	.75¢
Toilet paper	3 rolls	$1.50	90	.01¢	20	.20¢
Disinfectant	250 mL	$2.00	50	.04¢	7	.28¢
Toothpaste	100 mL	$1.20	30	.04¢	5	.20¢

Total supply cost per week __$1.43__

Total supply cost per week x 4 = Total supply cost per month

Total supply cost per month ÷ number of children in day care = supply cost per child per month

Complete Worksheet #9 to estimate your equipment replacement costs. Sample #5 shows Worksheet #9 completed for a fictional day care.

Ideally, from day one, you will put the money you estimate for equipment costs into a "replacement fund," so that when something does wear out or get broken, the funds will be there to replace it. This is smart, long-range business planning. At the least, make sure that you don't look at your lovely bank balance at the end of the year and think all that money is pure profit; it isn't, and you will be needing it when equipment wears out.

4. Other costs

Your other costs may include the following:

(a) Telephone

(b) Office supplies

(c) Insurance

(d) Loan repayment

(e) Advertising and promotion

(f) Professional services (accountant, lawyer)

(g) Rent

(h) Utilities

(i) Unemployment premiums

(j) Pension payments

(k) Vacation pay

(l) Medical insurance

(m) Social security

(n) Income taxes

Several of these costs, such as mortgage, telephone, and utilities, are expenses that you already pay for your personal use. Now that you will be using part of your own home to house your business, you should consider a percentage of those costs as expenses for your day care. Think of it as renting part of your home to your business. You can use a square-footage method to decide how much of your rent or utilities is a business expense. For example, if your rent is $1,000 per month, your house approximately 1,000 square feet, and the area that you devote exclusively to child care is approximately 300 square feet, you might consider $300 per month to be your rental costs. Other costs can also be calculated based on the percentage of use by your business.

Note: calculating prorated business expenses is a complicated area. Be sure to check with your accountant regarding legitimate business expenses before deducting any prorated costs as business expenses.

5. Total expense estimate

You are now in a position to estimate the bulk of your expenses. Add together the total food cost per month, the total supply cost per month, the total equipment cost per month, and the other costs per month. This will give you a total expenses per month figure (see Worksheet #10). Now, you can subtract your estimated expenses from your income and see how much profit you will be making each month.

WORKSHEET #9
EQUIPMENT REPLACEMENT COST ANALYSIS

Item	Price	Estimated lifetime (in years)	Cost per year	Cost per month

Total equipment cost per month_____

Total equipment cost ÷ number of children in day care =
Equipment cost per child per month

SAMPLE #5
EQUIPMENT REPLACEMENT COST ANALYSIS

Item	Price	Estimated lifetime (in years)	Cost per year	Cost per month
Toothbrush	$1.20	3 months	$4.80	40¢
Scissors	$2.50	1	$2.50	21¢
Juicer	$80.00	1	$80.00	$6.65
Paintbrush	$2.00	6 months	$4.00	33¢
Facecloths	$2.50	1	$2.50	21¢
Games	$20.00	1	$20.00	$1.67
Chair	$15.00	2	$7.50	63¢
Toys	$10.00	6 months	$20.00	$1.67

Total equipment cost per month___$11.77

Total equipment cost ÷ number of children in day care =
Equipment cost per child per month

WORKSHEET #10
ESTIMATED OPERATING BUDGET

INCOME

      Child care food program   _____

      Subsidies   _____

      Parent fees   _____

TOTAL   _____

EXPENSES

      Food   _____

      Supplies   _____

      Equipment   _____

      Office supplies   _____

      Telephone   _____

      Office supplies   _____

      Insurance   _____

      Loan repayments   _____

      Income taxes   _____

      Advertising and promotion   _____

      Accountant's fees   _____

      Lawyer's fees   _____

      Rent   _____

      Utilities   _____

      Unemployment premiums   _____

      Pension payments   _____

      Vacation pay   _____

      Medical insurance   _____

      Social security   _____

      Miscellaneous   _____

TOTAL EXPENSES   _____

PROFIT   _____

Fun Time Cheese Balls

1 small package cream cheese

1 tsp. salad dressing

- Combine cream cheese and salad dressing mixture into balls.
- Roll mixture into sesame seeds or bread crumbs.
- Goes great with pretzel sticks or bread sticks.

6

SETTING YOUR RATES

What should you charge for child care? There are several factors to consider when you are working out your rates, including the following:

(a) the local standard,

(b) your expenses,

(c) your time, and

(d) your quality of care.

None of these factors alone can tell you how much to charge; you need to look at all of them together. For example, it is dangerous to simply decide that the average rate charged in your area is x amount, so you will charge x amount, too. If your expenses are greater than the others' or there is some other factor you are not aware of, you may end up running your business at a loss! Similarly, you can't simply work out your expenses and then base your rates accordingly without looking into what the market will bear. You need to look at all factors, then adjust your rates, your expenses, or your time commitment to make sure that you are making a reasonable profit.

a. LOCAL RATE STANDARDS

Call several day cares advertised in your Yellow Pages or in the newspaper to get an idea of what an average rate is. You do not want to go below these basic rates because, in the end, the lack of profit will have a direct impact on your ability to provide optimum care. Placing your rates too high, on the other hand, may prevent you from maintaining full capacity, which will also bring your profits down. In the end, the results are the same.

In most instances, you will find that rates charged for part-time care tend to be slightly higher than for full-time care. Some day cares have a reduced fee for a second or third child, and many offer to work with government subsidy programs for low-income families. Your state or provincial licensing office can give you more information on who to contact about subsidy programs.

Use the first part of Worksheet #11 to work out the average rates for your area. Sample #6 shows how this would be done.

b. YOUR EXPENSES

When calculating your rates, you will need to look at the expense estimate you did in chapter 5. This way you can make sure that your rates cover your expenses as well as paying you a salary. Remember that your expenses should be calculated on a per child per month basis if your rates are monthly.

c. YOUR TIME

Your time is your greatest asset. After all, if you didn't want to run a day care, you could, presumably, sell your time to an employer. So take a look at how much time you will be putting into your new business before setting your rates.

Estimate how many hours you will be putting in per week, for example, if you are open from 8:30 to 5:30, you are working 45 hours per week. On top of this, you may need to do some record keeping or shopping, so add two hours per week. If you decide you need to make at least $8 per hour, you will need to make $376 per week above

WORKSHEET #11
AVERAGE DAY-CARE RATES

Day Care	First child				Second child				Late pickup-fee	Extra charges
	Monthly	Weekly	Daily	Hourly	Monthly	Weekly	Daily	Hourly		
#1										
#2										
#3										
#4										
#5										
TOTALS										
Divide totals by 5 to get average rates										
Average rates										

SAMPLE #6
AVERAGE DAY-CARE RATES

Day Care	First child				Second child				Late pickup-fee	Extra charges
	Monthly	Weekly	Daily	Hourly	Monthly	Weekly	Daily	Hourly		
#1	$1500	$375	$75	$8.33	$1400	$350	$70	$7.78	$10	$5
#2	$1600	$400	$80	$8.89	$1400	$350	$70	$7.78	$15	$10
#3	$1400	$350	$70	$7.78	$1300	$325	$65	$7.22	$10	$5
#4	$1200	$300	$60	$6.67	$1200	$300	$60	$6.67	$15	$10
#5	$1300	$325	$65	$7.22	$1300	$325	$65	$7.22	$15	$10
TOTALS	$7000	$1750	$350	$38.89	$6600	$1650	$330	$36.67	$65	$40
Divide totals by 5 to get average rates	$7000/5	$1750/5	$350/5	$38.89/5	$6600/5	$1650/5	$330/5	$36.67/5	$65/5	$40/5
Average rates	$1400	$350	$70	$7.78	$1320	$330	$66	$7.33	$13	$8

56

and beyond your expenses. If you take in three children, you will need to charge $376 ÷ 3 or approximately $125 per child per week just to cover your time costs.

Of course, many business owners don't think in terms of paying themselves an hourly wage; they concentrate on overall profits. However, working it out with an hourly wage will at least give you an idea of how much you will be making compared to other jobs you could be doing.

d. YOUR QUALITY OF CARE

Now that you have looked at what other day cares charge and considered your expenses and time costs, you have a good concept of what base rates for child care should be. Your next step is to ask yourself if you are really worth more than the base rate.

Your training and experience may justify charging a slightly higher rate since many parents will opt for paying extra fees if the provider is worth it. The same holds true for your program. If you offer a greater variety of outings or bring in specialized help (e.g., a professional storyteller, dance instructor, or craft leader), your customers can expect to pay a bit more.

A higher fee, usually $10 to $20 per week, is often charged for infants, as babies require more individual care and require a higher staff/child ratio.

e. LATE FEES

You will also have to decide on overtime fees or late pick-up fees, which can be charged by the minute or the quarter hour. Caregivers have taken to charging these fees in self-defense against parents who are continually and unnecessarily late in picking up their children. In some cases, caregivers charge $10 for each 15 minutes a parent is late, while others charge $1 for every minute of overtime. Parents, when faced with these steep overtime bills, tend to be less tardy when it comes to retrieving their child. Hold your ground on this issue and you won't be walked on.

f. ABSENTEEISM

Charging parents a regular weekly rate, regardless of whether a child is absent on some days due to illness or whatever, will secure your income and simplify your record keeping. Do not be tempted to reduce a parent's fees for any absent days. After all, you cannot suddenly be absent and expect the parent to find and pay for a substitute caregiver. It is the same thing.

g. HOLIDAYS AND VACATIONS

Statutory holidays should be included in all parent fees and are so when a weekly or monthly rate is charged.

Summer holidays present another issue to be discussed with the parents. Most employers begin planning annual holiday schedules by the first of March. Ask parents to let you know when they have booked their vacation time so you can plan your summer or holiday activities according to the numbers and ages of the children who will be in your care. You also need to know what income you are working with on a monthly basis to prepare budget sheets.

Some day cares require parents to pay even for the weeks that they take the children out of day care to go on vacation. The rationale is that the caregiver is not likely to find another child to fill that space for those exact weeks and he or she is really "holding" that space for the child that is coming back. If you take this approach, you can explain to parents that this actually allows them more flexibility, as they can take their vacations whenever they want without having to coordinate their schedules with that of the caregiver. As the space will be paid for whether or not the child is there, the parent can arrange the vacation any time.

You will also have to decide how you will handle your own vacation time. Will you provide an alternate caregiver or simply shut down during that period? If you plan to shut down, you will have to plan your vacations far in advance so that parents can make alternate arrangements for the children.

h. RATE INCREASES

Most centers increase their fees in September when school-age children are leaving the center and making room for new children. This is also a good time to schedule your yearly parent consultation (often required under legislation), as it allows you an opportunity to explain your reasons for increasing your rates. It also gives you an opportunity to show the parents how well little Johnny or Janey is doing under your care and how wonderfully he or she is progressing in social and developmental skills.

Though not required in all states and provinces, it is a good practice for your quality day care. In Nova Scotia, for example, the Day Care Act regulations say that —

> full day programs shall hold a parents' meeting not less than once every three months. The agenda shall be made available to parents and parents shall be permitted to add items to the agenda. Minutes of all parents' meetings are to be kept on file at the office of the family day care agency.

i. BAD ACCOUNTS

There may come a time, unfortunately, when a parent defaults on paying you. Being prepared to handle a situation of this nature may not make you feel any better, but it will give you the strength to fight for what is yours.

A bad check can be handled tactfully. Ask the parent to replace the check with the appropriate amount in cash, plus the service charge the bank levied on your account to return the check. A statement showing both these figures will leave little room for disputes. At this point, the parent should be told that you will only accept payment in the form of cash. Better yet, make this official and put it in writing in duplicate, with one copy for the parent and one copy attached to the parent's child-care agreement.

Late or overdue accounts call for more drastic measures such as interest charges or a statement of account that the parent receives no later than two days after the expired pay period. The statement should cover the amount of fees owed, the period that the fees cover, and the date the fees were due. On the statement you could also remind the parent of your interest charges of x% per week that the account is outstanding.

If a parent is reluctant to pay, discuss the situation calmly with him or her, inquiring about the possibility of working out a suitable payment schedule.

As a last measure, you must terminate the care and inform the parents you will take the matter up with the local credit bureau and will proceed to file suit in small claims court if necessary. For your own protection, you should see the problem through.

As you stumble through the first few months of your new venture, you'll learn a few techniques that can assist you in collecting the money you work so hard to earn. It may be as simple as putting little bills in the parents' information envelope a couple of days before payment is due, or placing a happy face sticker on the weekly calendar the day before payday. With a little creativity and a gentle reminder, you may never have to refer to the overdue account or bad check policy on your rate sheet.

j. THE RATE SHEET

Licensing requirements in most areas stipulate that rates must be posted clearly in a place where they can be referred to by parents. This is a good idea as it helps to remind parents that you are running a business and you take the business of caring for their children seriously. The rate sheet should include your policies regarding holidays, vacations, illness, unscheduled absent days, and when and how a parent is required to pay. You should clearly state your policy on overdue accounts and bad checks.

Also on your rate sheet should be your policy for termination of care, or more specifically, the amount of notification time you require when a child will no longer be part of your day care. Three to four weeks is an average request for a notification of termination of care. Parents who pull their children from your care without proper notification or a justifiable reason, should be charged a penalty — generally an amount covering the requested notice period.

Sample #7 is a typical rate sheet.

Magicland Day Care
Rate Information Sheet

The following rates are applicable to all families.

RATE SHEET	FULL TIME (per week)	PART TIME (per day)	CASUAL (per hour)
Infants, 1 - 12 months	$400	$23	$3
Toddlers, 12 - 24 months	$375	$20	$3
Preschool, 2 - 5 years	$350	$20	$3
School-age,	n/a	n/a	$3
Special Needs	$500	$25	$5
Long Day (10 1/2 - 12 hours)	$460	$25	n/a
After School	n/a	n/a	$3
Two Children Families	$700	$30	$4
Three Children Families	$800	$35	$4

Subsidy rates available - please inquire.

FEES: -Are DUE every FRIDAY, and are to be paid in cash or by check.

- Do not include the provision of diapers, formula, baby food, special diet foods which cannot be prepared by the day care. These are the parents' responsibility.

OVERTIME FEES: Parents will be granted a grace period of 15 minutes after their scheduled pick-up time, after which the following overtime rates apply: $1 per minute the parent is late. Overtime fees are to be paid when the parent arrives to pick up their child. The day care closes at 6:00 p.m. sharp. The 15-minute grace period does not apply to the facility closing time.

ABSENT DAYS: As full-time fees are based on a weekly rate, absent days when the child will not attend care due to illness, doctor appointment, parent day off, etc. will not be deducted from the rate.

The same policy applies for steady, part-time customers.

SUMMER HOLIDAYS: Parents are requested to notify the day care of their holiday plans by the end of May to allow for activity and budget planning. Parents will not be responsibile for their fees for 20 holiday days. Rates will be charged, in lieu of holding open the child's space, for any holidays taken after the 20 days.

STATUTORY HOLIDAYS: As listed below. The day care will not be open for care. These days, however, are included in the weekly fee and will not be deducted from the fee. Part-time customers who are scheduled for care on any statutory holiday will be paying their standard rate.

New Year's Day

Labor Day

Thanksgiving Day

Christmas Day

Boxing Day

ANNUAL INCREASES: Will be made, if necessary, on the 1st day of September. Parents will be notified in writing one month prior to this day of any increase in their normal rate.

PARENT CONSULTATIONS: Will be scheduled in August to discuss concerns, the child's development, program schedules, and rate increases.

TERMINATION OF CARE: Parents are required to submit to the day care three weeks' written notice of termination of care. Those providing less notice will still be required to pay for care for the full three-week term of notice.

In the event that after the trial period the provision of care (as outlined in our policy statement) is not deemed to be working out, the day care has the right, upon two weeks written notice to the parent, to terminate the care. All fees owing to the final date of care are to be paid on the final day on which care is provided.

HOURS OF OPERATION: Magicland Day Care is open from 6:30 a.m. until 6:00 p.m., Monday - Friday. Children will be accepted from 6:45 a.m. and must depart no later than 6:00 p.m. Overnight and/or weekend care is available by special arrangement only.

The day care will be closed on all statutory holidays. Care for these days will be by special arrangement also.

Skipping Songs

Another favorite game that has stood the test of time is jump rope. Remember these skipping songs?

Cinderella

Cinderella dressed in yellow,

Went upstairs to kiss a fellow,

By mistake she kissed a snake,

How many doctors did it take?

1, 2, 3, 4, 5, 6, 7, ...

Blondie and Dagwood

Two people turn the ends:

Blondie and Dagwood went downtown,

Blondie bought an evening gown,

Dagwood bought a new pair of shoes,

While Cookie stayed home and read the news,

And this is what it said:

Close your eyes and count to ten,

If you miss you take the end.

7

SETTING AND STATING POLICIES

It should be clear to you by now that you are, in essence, running a small business. This means it is your responsibility to set the guidelines by which you will operate and adhere to. Make no apologies for requesting parents to sign a child-care agreement, pay late pick-up charges, or pay you a certain percent (if not all) of the daily rate for unscheduled absent days, or for turning a family away after the trial period if you feel you cannot work effectively with the parents or the child. This is your business, your livelihood, and if you cannot enjoy it, then it will be the children who suffer.

However, you cannot expect parents to understand or adhere to policies that are not even clearly understood by you. So, your first step in getting your customers to follow policies is to define those policies for yourself.

a. WHAT AGE GROUP WILL YOU CARE FOR?

Children are a pure delight at any age. So how on earth are you to decide what age group to care for? Right now you may be thinking it doesn't really matter, but it does. Licensing regulations alone will control your options to some extent.

Let's put these regulations aside for a moment and have a look at which age groups you are equipped to handle, which groups fit with the ages of your own children, and which groups you will actually be more comfortable caring for on a daily basis.

Say, for example, you have a two-year-old and a four-year-old of your own who are highly mobile and energetic. At the moment, you are able to take them to the wave pool, the library, even shopping when the mood strikes you. Caring for an infant would severely restrict these activities. While you may be thinking it would be charming to have a baby around to cuddle and coddle, will you feel the same when your children want to go swimming and you have to say no because it is the baby's nap time? Or how about the noise children create when they are playing? How will it affect the baby's nap?

If you are the parent of an infant, you might feel more relaxed caring for another infant and perhaps one older child with whom you can spend personal time when the babies are napping. If you have a child who has just grown out of the need for a crib and jolly jumper, but you still have all that baby-oriented equipment, you might be ideally set up to take on an infant. On the other hand, if your own children are long past that stage and you would have to go out and buy all the paraphernalia associated with infants, you might think twice about the expense involved.

If you still feel it doesn't matter what age of child you care for, consider the age of children you enjoy most. Do you like the hectic lifestyle of feedings and diaper changes interspersed with the relaxation of nap times, or do you fancy walks in the park and building a snowman, something that may be more difficult to do when an infant is around? Are you very much a homebody who prefers the sweet giggles of a baby or do you like the freedom to gather up the clan and head off to the beach for an afternoon of water tag and sun?

To help you arrive at a decision, let's look at some of the advantages and disadvantages of caring for children of different ages.

Advantages

- Infant nap times allow you to be more actively involved with the older children.

- Children will learn to get along with not only their peers, but children of different ages and development levels.

- Children will learn from each other. By watching the older children, the younger ones will be eager to learn the alphabet, tie shoes, and be involved in more developed games.

- Older children learn to be patient as they wait for the younger ones to get dressed or changed.

- Older children become more responsible and independent. They may have to take care of themselves while you are changing the baby or they may want to help you. Older children learn to take care of the younger ones by playing with them or helping feed them.

- A group of children of different ages, or a "blended household," as it is sometimes called, offers more of a family-like setting.

Disadvantages

- Your time may not be equally divided between the different age groups. For example, infants require frequent feedings and diaper changes. Their schedules may interrupt the art project or other activities you have planned for the older children.

- An older child's need to be on the go, both indoors and out, may be restricted by an infant's immobility.

- Field trips may be more difficult to arrange if you have to plan around an infant's schedule.

- Older children may resent the time you spend caring for the younger children.

Consider your tolerance level. Can you handle a crying baby? Will toys strewn in disarray about your home bother you? Are you prepared to handle an active two-year-old? What is it about children at the infant, toddler and preschool level age that bothers you? What do you like about particular age groups? Weigh your answers carefully. Are you capable of arranging activities for the different age groups or do you prefer to read through a story uninterrupted, or can you tolerate the inability of a toddler to sit still long enough for you to get to the story's end?

So many questions, but they all reflect your feelings about children. There is absolutely nothing wrong with being selective in the ages of the children you choose to care for. In fact, the children will be better off because you will be comfortable with both them and your arrangements.

Nonetheless, if a blended household appeals to you and you enjoy the challenges that come with caring for children of different ages, there are many things you can do to achieve a balanced program for all. Walks, trips to the park, art activities, even house cleaning can be enjoyed by one and all. It simply takes a little more planning.

Whatever your choice is, you should have the decision made before you begin to advertise your services, allowing you to target your advertising to the parents of a particular age group. This will save you answering pointless calls about children you cannot accommodate.

If you are asked to provide care for a child who is not of an age you are willing to or have the proper equipment to care for, resist the temptation to bring that child into your care. The problems may prove too many and it is not good for a child to begin bonding to you and your family, only to have these bonds severed. Children need the security of a steady environment and a person they know they can trust.

b. HOW MANY CHILDREN CAN YOU ACCOMMODATE?

As we discussed in chapter 3, licensing regulations govern the number of children of a particular age that one person can care for. And rightly so. These restrictions are created with a child's safety and well-being in mind. Without such rules and regulations it might be tempting for a caregiver to take on "just one more child" — and that one might be one more than she can handle. Soon, accidents are occurring, children are neglected, television is used as a pacifier, and the overall health standard declines because the provider is unable to perform even the simplest of housekeeping duties. The result would be a very poor quality of child care, and the child is the one who suffers.

So, from reading your licensing regulations, you know the maximum number of children you can legally take in. However, you still have to decide if you can or want to accommodate that many.

The size of your home or apartment will affect the number of children you can care for. A home has only so much living room and kitchen space. Consider how many children can crawl, toddle, or run about its perimeters comfortably. How many children can you sit at your kitchen table for arts and crafts and for meals?

How about your backyard? Is the play space restricted because of a double garage or large storage sheds, or is there ample space for a number of children to romp around? How many children do you feel the space can accommodate? Remember, outside equipment such as swings, tricycles, a sandbox, and a picnic table take up considerable space. How will this affect your play area?

If you have any concerns about the number of children you will be able to care for effectively, start out small. It is easier to take on more children if it seems feasible than to terminate the care of the "one too many" you took on.

c. HOW WILL YOU HANDLE THE ILLNESS OF A CHILD?

Because there are hundreds of viruses around and because children have not built up an immunity to these viruses, your charges will get sick, and you have to make some serious decisions as to when you will and will not provide care for a sick child. This is a difficult decision because, while you want to accommodate parents whenever you can, there are health risks to the other children, your family, and yourself if you allow a sick child into your care. Just how do you decide when *sick* is simply *too sick*?

The best person to answer this question is the public health nurse. He or she can help you work out a reasonable policy concerning illness. The nurse can give you suggestions on how to isolate a sick child, what important signs to watch for that could indicate a serious health problem, the general rules about when to seek help for a high fever, and which diseases are highly contagious and require you to either refuse care or to help parents seek sick care.

Your day-care licensing board probably has its own rules regarding when a child is too ill to be in care. But these are only guidelines, so unless you have an understanding of childhood illnesses and how infectious these can be, you'll have a great deal of difficulty maintaining any type of disease control in your day care.

1. Communicable diseases

Communicable diseases are a common problem in any setting where children gather. Again, the public health nurse can help you recognize these diseases. He or she will also give you guidelines to follow on dealing with these diseases, when a child should be discharged, and when the child will be ready for re-admission to the center. The nurse can give you tips on when and how you should notify parents of any communicable diseases or viruses affecting the other children in the center or home.

2. Administering medication

Many providers accept a child into care who is mildly ill with a cold or slight cough. Caring for mildly ill children may, however, involve the administering of medicine such as cough syrup or antibiotics. You will be responsible for setting your own policy as to whether you choose to administer medicine, or whether you would prefer a parent make other arrangements (such as setting the medication times for before and after the child is in day care).

If you do take on the responsibility of medicating a child, be sure to have the parents complete a medication permission form such as the one shown in Sample #16 in chapter 12.

For more on handling health issues, see chapter 12.

d. HOW WILL YOU ORGANIZE TRANSPORTATION AND FIELD TRIPS?

Many day cares undertake some form of transportation of the children in their care. Some transport school-age children to and from school, others pick up the children from the parent's home or workplace and then return them there at a designated time. These are known as routine trips or regularly scheduled excursions. Then there are those day cares who take the children on field trips or special outings.

Regardless of the frequency of the transportation, there are certain procedures that should be followed. Your licensing body will undoubtedly have regulations concerning transportation. Be sure you study and adhere to them carefully.

For your own use and for each trip, you should have a written plan that includes the following:

(a) The means of transportation

(b) The name and position of the driver or person in charge

(c) The approximate arrival and departure times

(d) The rules that will be enforced, for example —

   (i) children will wear seat belts or be installed in proper child restraint

  (ii) children will enter and exit the vehicle on the curb side of the road

 (iii) children will keep one hand on the side of the vehicle until being told otherwise

 (iv) children will hold hands when walking to the bus stop

(e) The pick-up and drop-off locations

(f) The procedures that are to be followed if a child is late or missing from the designated pick-up location

This plan makes it clear to both you and the parent what will be done, when, and how.

In addition, whether the transportation is regular or only used for field trips, you must have a signed and dated permission form from the parent before any child is transported to or from the center or home (see Sample #8). This permission form must include —

(a) the child's name,

(b) the pick-up and drop-off locations (for regular trips),

(c) the pick-up and drop-off times

(d) the destination(s),

(e) the date(s) or days on which the trip(s) will take place,

(f) the signature of the parent, and

(g) the date the form was signed.

e. WHAT KIND OF BEHAVIOR MANAGEMENT (DISCIPLINE) WILL YOU USE?

Discipline, according to *Webster's College Dictionary*, means "1. training to act in accordance with rules... 2. activity, exercise or a regimen that develops or improves a skill; training." It is derived from the word *disciple*, meaning a pupil who adheres to certain teachings. No matter what you call it — discipline, behavior management, or child guidance — it in no way connotes punishment.

As a provider of child care, you are assuming the role of a teacher. You teach children how to walk, how to count, how to go potty, how to get along with other children, and so on. You are also responsible for teaching them what is and what is not acceptable behavior. And just as developing intellectual, emotional, and physical skills is an ongoing, continuous process, so is learning appropriate behavior.

When a child is learning to walk, he or she must, by the very laws of nature, take a few tumbles along the way. In time, the child not only learns to walk, but to run, skip, and jump. The path down the road to behavior management also has many potholes, hills, and its fair share of forks that lead to both correct and incorrect actions. It is the caregiver's responsibility to help the child through the rough spots, to pick him or her up when a mistake is made, and to help the child decide which fork in the road will be the best path to follow.

As philosophical as all this may sound, it should set the premise on which you establish your policies regarding discipline. For although your licensing regulations tell you what you cannot do to discipline a child, they do not tell you which disciplinary practices you should employ. It is up to you to learn more about child guidance and discipline issues and to define your rules for behavior and behavior management.

Caring for Children in Your Home, a handbook produced by the Ohio Department of Human Services, recommends these three simple rules for children to govern their behavior:

● You may not hurt yourself.

● You may not hurt others. (Hurt can be emotional too, not just physical.)

● You may not hurt things (furniture, toys, etc.)

Keep in mind that whatever rules you do create for the children, they must —

(a) be easy for the children to understand

(b) be easy to explain to the children

(c) state limits in a very positive way, and

(d) encourage caring and cooperation.

Discipline is not an easy issue to deal with. There are, of course, forms of discipline that are definitely taboo and should be avoided completely. These include slapping or spanking a child, shaking, shouting (except to get a child's immediate attention), and embarrassing or humiliating a child in front of his or her peers. These methods do nothing to help a child see how his or her behavior is inappropriate.

Instead, you should consider implementing a discipline policy that contains all, or a combination of, the following techniques:

SAMPLE #8
TRANSPORTATION PERMISSION FORM

I hereby authorize _____ to
transport my son/daughter,_____ , by
_____ to and from _____
on the following days _____.

I acknowledge the pick-up time to be_____,
and the drop-off time to be_____.
I acknowledge the pick-up location to be_____
and the drop-off location to be_____

Date: _____

Parent's signature:_____

_____

I hereby authorize _____ to
transport my son/daughter,_____ , by
_____ to and from _____
on the following days _____.

I acknowledge the pick-up time to be_____,
and the drop-off time to be_____.
I acknowledge the pick-up location to be_____
and the drop-off location to be_____

Date: _____

Parent's signature:_____

- Praise a child's appropriate behavior. A smile, a hug, a soft kiss on the cheek tell children that you appreciate their thoughtfulness, their helping out, their wonderful attitude. By building children's self-esteem, you reinforce appropriate behavior. Deep down children want to please us; let them know when they have.

- Be consistent in enforcing your rules. Let the children know the reason for the rule: "We don't lean back on the chairs because we can fall and hurt ourselves," or "We don't pull the cat's tail because she will get mad and scratch us."

- Direct your messages to the behavior and in such a way that you don't put the child down. Rather than saying "No, you are not wearing your shoes in the rain. I don't care how much you cry," say "Rain boots keep your feet dry so you don't catch cold. Shoes won't work today." Instead of saying "You don't take things away from other people like that," say "Taking Jane's crayon makes her cry and feel bad."

- Set reasonable limitations. Children do not know or understand what is expected unless they are taught. Guide them gently and patiently as they learn to share, respect other's feelings, and acquire good manners. It won't happen overnight; chances are that you will have to look the other way occasionally as long as no one is getting hurt.

- Let the children know what you expect of them in a positive way. "It's time to wash up before lunch," works better than "Hurry up kids, if you don't wash up soon you won't get any lunch." Say "Babies need you to be gentle with them," rather than "Don't poke the baby like that; it's bad."

In situations where immediate action is required you can —

- distract the child by showing him or her something else to play with instead of the ball they so desperately want from another child,

- gently touch the child's shoulder or put an arm around his or her waist; this often calms the child and allows you to redirect his or her attention. Sometimes a tight hug is soothing.

- let the children know you understand their feelings before you correct their behavior: "I know it's hard for you to wait for your turn on the tricycle, but everyone will get a turn before we go inside."

- impose a time-out when a child refuses to obey the house rules. The time-out area should be far enough from the play area to calm the child down. You can use a timer to let the child know when he or she may reenter the play area. The rule of thumb is one minute of time-out for each year of the child's age. Avoid using corners or asking a child to sit facing the wall.

- hold or hug the child when he or she throws a tantrum. This helps calm the child and helps the child learn self-control. Holding lets the child know that you are supportive. You can discuss the problem with the child and help him or her to understand ways to deal with the problem in future.

There may come a time when a child refuses to abide by your rules or is a threat to both him or herself and to the other children. This child is "hard to manage" and you should plan ahead of time how to handle this situation. You must tell the parents and get their assistance. This will not be easy for either of you.

To smooth the way, set up an appointment to talk with both parents together. Here are some tips to make this easier for all involved:

- The best way to start is to tell the parents the child's good points and any progress he or she is making.

- Then describe the behavior you have witnessed and ask how they deal with similar situations at home. Never accuse them of being bad parents or tell them their child is "totally irresponsible and uncontrollable." Let the behavior speak for itself.

- If the parents have the same problem, ask them what steps they have taken to correct the inappropriate behavior. If nothing has been done, ask how they plan to help their child.

- At this point it is best to set a deadline for the parents to seek help or by which you feel the behavior should be corrected. Keep tabs on the situation by requesting notes from the child's doctor or specialist. It is the parents' responsibility to seek help and support for their child.

- If the parents refuse to get help and/or the situation does not improve, you may have to ask the parents to remove the child from your care before another child gets hurt or your program suffers.

For more information on child discipline, the Independent Order of Foresters has a number of booklets that deal with the issue. Write to:

The Independent Order of Foresters
100 Border Avenue
Solana Beach, CA 92075

or

The Independent Order of Foresters
789 Don Mills Road
Don Mills, Ontario
M3C 1T9

f. WHAT KIND OF SUPPLIES WILL PARENTS PROVIDE?

You need to decide what kind of supplies the parents will be responsible for providing, even if it's simply a change of clothing or an extra jacket.

This is particularly true when it comes to diapers. Some day cares require parents to supply diapers (cloth or disposable) and take away soiled cloth diapers, while others, to avoid hassles or being caught in short supply, purchase the diapers themselves and incorporate the cost into their fees. You should do what feels comfortable, but keep in mind that many state and provincial licensing boards are very strict with their rules concerning diapering. You should review your licensing requirements before you make any decision.

g. WHO WILL ACT AS SUBSTITUTE CAREGIVERS?

It's inevitable, it's unavoidable, and it's Murphy's Law. People get sick, have accidents, and require time off from work for various reasons. Needless to say, you are going to have to find substitute caregivers to take over for those occasions.

Before you open your door to care you should have, at minimum, two persons you can call upon at any time to help you out. This may prove a difficult task because substitute child-care workers are in short supply, and even when you do find one or two, there is no guarantee they will be available when you need them. The law of supply and demand is not always a fair one.

Many states and provinces require you to post the names and telephone numbers of your substitutes and give parents a copy of this information as well. Some also insist that all substitute caregivers sign a written statement certifying their availability and agreement to serve as substitutes. These agreements must be kept on file.

Whenever possible, you should have the substitute come into your home, allowing you to introduce him or her to the children and the parents. This way, when you do have to be absent, the substitute will not be a total stranger to the children. It will also give you a chance to show the substitute around your home, explain your policies and emergency procedures, familiarize him or her with your program and daily schedules, and get to know him or her better. Treating your sub fairly and like part of the family will help you to hang on to him or her.

The Child Care Employee Project (CCEP) has produced an informative booklet called *A Good Sub is Hard to Find* that is full of valuable tips on locating substitute caregivers and establishing a substitute referral system. To obtain a copy of this booklet, write to: Child Care Employee Project, 6536 Telegraph Avenue, Suite A201, Oakland, CA 94609-1114.

h. WHO WILL YOU RELEASE THE CHILD TO?

Another area of concern will be arrangements for releasing the child from your care. This may sound simple, but once the child is given into your care, you are responsible for making sure he or she is only released into the proper hands. For example, you don't want to get caught in the middle of a situation where an estranged spouse turns up one day to pick the child up; you, all unknowing, release the child to him or her, and the parent with custody becomes angry at you for releasing the child to the other parent.

You will need to discuss exactly what arrangements each parent wishes to make for his or her child. A typical arrangement might allow you to release the child to —

(a) either parent,

(b) a predesignated emergency contact person, or

(c) any other guardian authorized in writing by the parent.

If neither the parent nor any other person named on the release portion of your child care agreement is able to pick the child up, the parent must give you as much notification and information as possible *in writing* about the change in plans and about the person to whom you are to release the child.

Do not be tempted to do without these safeguards; the safety of the child is at stake and if you cannot get these assurances, you are much better off to hold the child safe in your care until someone with the proper authorization does show up.

i. HOW WILL YOU ENCOURAGE PARENTAL PARTICIPATION?

Parent participation encompasses a variety of activities, some regulated by licensing bodies and some left to your discretion.

You have to tell parents what their rights are in your day care and allow them the freedom to act on those rights. One licensing office may dictate the establishment of a parent advisory council and outline the exact responsibility of the council. Another may merely require operators to hold yearly parent conferences and to allow parents unlimited access to all areas of the center where the care is provided. Review your local regulations and be sure that your policies reflect them.

Of course, you want to encourage parent participation in any case because research shows that the quality of care increases when parents take an active role in the provision of that care. There are many ways to encourage parental involvement. For example, you could —

(a) hand out written daily reports on a child's physical well-being, achievements, or special activity;

(b) talk to parents to find out their interests and hobbies and ask if they would share these with the children;

(c) ask parents for their help during field trips, birthday parties, religious holidays, or cultural activities;

(d) run an open house or drop-in-evening once a month to encourage parents to pop around after hours if they have any concerns or problems they would like to discuss, or to offer parenting seminars, educational videos, and group discussions;

(e) open a parent library or resource center;

(f) set up a parent bulletin board;

(g) establish a parent advisory council, offering parents a meaningful role in the governance of your center; or

(h) call parents after hours to let them know how their child is doing, especially if something wonderful happened and you forgot to mention it when the parent came to pick up the child.

For more on parental involvement, see chapter 15.

j. WHAT ARE YOUR EMERGENCY PROCEDURES?

When an emergency occurs is not the right time to be formulating policies on how to handle the situation. Before a single child steps into your home, you should establish the procedures you will follow in the event of an accident, fire, or if a child becomes seriously ill. It is crucial that you have the procedures worked out and that you practice them monthly with the children and anyone else who will be in your home.

The single most important thing you can do to prepare yourself to handle emergencies is to take a first aid and a CPR course. The Red Cross, St. John Ambulance, and many local community colleges offer these life-saving courses. Make an appointment

to attend one now. Your ability to respond quickly in an emergency can literally mean the difference between life and death.

k. WHEN WILL YOU PROVIDE CARE?

Ask yourself what days of the week and what hours of each day you want to be available. Some day cares are open Monday to Friday, 6:30 a.m. to 6:00 p.m.. This would cover the needs of the typical working parent. However, many parents work shifts or weekends. Do you want to accommodate these families? Would you be willing to take in children overnight, say two nights a week, while a parent works night shift? What about taking in children in the evening while parents go out? Is it worth your while to accept a child for a few hours while the parents are at the theater or shopping?

Only you can answer these questions, keeping your own family needs and schedule in mind. However, you do need to make decisions about when you will be available *before* you start talking to prospective customers. Otherwise you may find yourself accommodating everyone else at the cost of your own lifestyle.

Realizing that you will not be able to fulfill the needs of every family will help you lighten the load created by your great expectations of being the best child-care provider the industry has ever known. The only honor you should be aiming for is the one that comes when you reach your goals without sacrificing your integrity or losing your mind.

l. WHAT MEALS WILL YOU PROVIDE?

Are you prepared to feed the children breakfast or will you insist that the children have had their breakfast before arriving? Will parents be responsible for furnishing their child with snacks? When will the children be eating? These are a few of the questions you need to consider when deciding on a meal policy. It is probably easiest for you to create your weekly menus and post them where parents can review them, rather than trying to post the menus daily.

Chapter 13 deals with nutrition and meal planning in more detail.

m. YOUR POLICY STATEMENT

Now that you have established to your own satisfaction what your policies will be, you need to put those policies down in writing. Doing this will accomplish two things. First, you will create a document for your own reference to ensure that you enforce your policies consistently and fairly. Second, you will provide yourself with a valuable communication tool to let others, particularly parents, know how you run your business, what you expect of them, and what they can expect of you.

If your plans are to help any parent regardless of the hours involved, say so in your policy. If you are only open for certain time periods and will not provide care outside of those hours, make that clear. If your goal is to provide specialized care for special-needs children, say so. If you are planning to give a home-like setting to a few children, that should go in your policy statement.

Formulate your policy statement carefully, for it will be the foundation of your day-to-day operations. It must apply to each parent and child who comes to you for child care and you must be willing to enforce it, no matter what.

As with almost everything you do in preparation for opening your door to child care, your licensing board will probably have something to say about your policy statement. Many authorities stipulate that you must have a policy statement, that each parent must receive a copy of this statement, and that a copy must be posted clearly on your information board, in your reception area, or anywhere else it may be conspicuous to parents.

Your policy statement should include a clear explanation of all the policies you decided on in sections **a.** through **l.** above. The rest of this chapter and Sample #9 will provide specific examples of items that should be included in your policy statement as well as sample wording for them.

1. Purpose and philosophy statement

Child care is more than simply putting a bunch of kids in a room and letting them play. The purpose and philosophy section of your policy statement allows you to express your personal philosophy in running your day care. Your philosophy statement should express your feelings and aspirations for your day care as they pertain to the children and their families. Share with everyone your dream of how you want your day care to operate.

The best place to include your statement of philosophy and purpose is at the very beginning of your policy statement, right after the name, address, and telephone number of your facility, before you get down to the specific terms and conditions that apply to your daily operations.

Your philosophy of child care should be the base that underlies every decision you make with regard to your day care, so make sure that your philosophy statement and your policies go together.

For example, if your philosophy statement emphasizes your belief in free expression, creativity, and flexibility, your policies should not reflect a regimentation and routine that would be at home in a military academy! On the other hand, some parents would probably feel happy leaving their children in an environment that is very structured and based on routine, so if that is going to be your approach, why not say so in your philosophy statement? No matter what your philosophy, you will probably find many people who share it. Be open about the kind of care you plan to provide; both you and the parent will be happier.

SAMPLE #9
POLICY STATEMENT

POLICY & PROCEDURES STATEMENT OF

MAGICLAND DAY CARE

2323 Main Street

Yourtown, Ontario   V0B 1C0

555-5672

Dear Parents,

This policy statement and the information contained herein was written in an effort to better acquaint you with The Magicland Daycare Center, our goals, and our commitment to the families we serve.

Purpose and philosophy

Magicland Day Care is dedicated to providing a warm and inviting atmosphere that allows children to develop at their own pace. We believe that children need to have a positive self-image. We foster that image, along with their developmental growth in the areas of intellectual, social, physical, and emotional skills, through a variety of group activities, individual play, and quiet periods. Our program makes use of many play and learning materials that help the children gain confidence in their abilities to do and make things. At Magicland Day Care, we are parent-friendly. We welcome parent visits anytime, and we seriously consider all parent suggestions and comments.

Age grouping and group size

Magicland Day Care is designed and licensed to care for a maximum of _____ children. We provide care for children ages two through five years. To enhance the quality of the care we provide, we have limited the number of children in each group and are following strict guidelines to maintain the staff/child ratios as set out by the licensing board. (A copy of our license is hanging in the reception area just above the Parent Information Board.)

Trial period

Because we are dedicated to providing only quality care, and because we care deeply for all children, there may be times, unfortunately, when the care we provide is not suitable for certain children or families. Therefore, we must be very stringent in imposing a trial period of three weeks, after which, if we deem the care inappropriate for the child for whatever reasons, we will decline from providing that care. If, regrettably, we must decline the provision of care, we will do what we can to help the parent find alternate care. However, the burden to find alternate care rests solely with the parent.

Parents will be given three weeks' notice of termination of care to allow them to search for alternate care.

Respectfully, if a parent feels the care we provide is not suited to their child or their family, the parent also has the right, after or during the three-week trial period, to terminate the care.

Meals and Snacks

We are committed to providing healthy meals and snacks for the children based on the federal food guides. These meals, (breakfast and lunch) will include one-third the daily totals in all four food groups. Snacks will be served of fruits, vegetables, or whole grain products. With the exception of the rare, special occasion, junk foods will not be served. Parents are asked to refrain from sending such foods as sweets, candies, or gums with their child.

Supplies and Equipment

The Magicland Daycare Center prides itself on its well-stocked toy and reading and arts area. WITH THE EXCEPTION OF A CHANGE OF WEATHER-RELATED CLOTHING, WHICH EVERY CHILD MUST HAVE AT THE CENTER, it is a rare occasion when parents are asked to help us to keep our supplies up. If by chance we require any additional supplies or equipment from the parents, we will put these requests in writing and will set a date by which these items will be required.

Emergencies

Emergency telephone numbers are posted at each telephone, as are our emergency evacuation plans. Parents are requested to go over these plans. Once a month the children and the staff will practice these fire, emergency, and severe weather evacuation plans.

In the event of a serious accident or illness, the parent will be contacted immediately. If the parent is not available we will notify the emergency contact person of the problem. Parents MUST fill out a CHILD MEDICAL REPORT, and an EMERGENCY MEDICAL CARE PERMISSION FORM, which will allow The Magicland Daycare Center to seek emergency aid for their child.

Any child who receives a minor cut or bruise will be tended to by first aid certified personnel. A report of such accidents will be filled out by the staff member in attendance, and one copy of the report will go to the parent and one copy will be placed in the injured child's file.

Illness

We are under very strict guidelines with regards to disease control, hence there may be times when we are either forced to send an ill child home, or not to accept an ill child into care. For that reason parents would be wise to have a plan for alternate care. If a child becomes ill at the center, we will do everything possible to comfort the child until the parent or emergency contact person arrives to take the child home. The child will have to be isolated from the other children.

Parents will be notified and required to remove the child immediately if a child exhibits any of the following symptoms:

Fever of 101° F (38.5° C).

Persistent diarrhea

Severe coughing

Difficult or rapid breathing

Conjunctivitis

Unusual spots or rashes

Vomiting

Yellowish color or tint to the eyes or skin (jaundice)

Difficulty in swallowing

Any other symptoms which, in the opinion of the caregiver, indicate the possible presence of a contagious disease such as chicken pox, measles, impetigo, etc.

Parents will be notified of contagious diseases affecting the children at the center. A child with a communicable disease will NOT be re-admitted into care until the period of contamination is passed or until the child is fully recovered from his or her illness.

Parents of all children in care are required to complete and submit to the caregiver a child medical report.

When medication, either prescription or over the counter, is involved in the child's care, the parent MUST fill out, sign and date a PERMISSION TO ADMINISTER MEDICATION FORM. These are to be filled out for each and every medicine.

Transportation and Field Trips

As a special service to parents, The Magicland Daycare Center will transport our school-age children to and from the following neighborhood schools: _____, _____, _____. In order for a child to take part in this program, parents MUST complete, sign and date a TRANSPORTATION PERMISSION FORM.

We also like to take the children on a variety of field trips. In order for us to do so we first need the parents' permission. Parents will therefore be notified in writing of any planned field trips, and will be required to complete, sign and date a TRANSPORTATION PERMISSION FORM (FIELD TRIP) for each outing. Failure to do so will mean the child will not be permitted to take part in this activity and will have to remain at the center.

ALL children MUST obey the following transportation rules: (1) children are to wear appropriate seat restraints, (2) children are to leave the vehicle on the curb side of the road only, (3) once outside the vehicle, children must stay beside this vehicle, keeping one hand on the side of the vehicle at all times, and (4) when preparing to enter or exit the vehicle, the children are to line up in an orderly fashion to be accounted for. Parents are to be sure their child understands these rules.

Ms. _____ is our transportation coordinator.

Behavior Management

The staff at The Magicland Daycare Center believe that children need guidance, understanding, and a few easy-to-follow rules in order to learn appropriate behavior. It is our policy to help children learn appropriate behavior by establishing clear limits, explaining those limits in a positive way when it is necessary for a child to understand why the limit is there, by using the time-out method to calm a child when necessary. We believe a one minute per the child's age is a sufficient time-out period.

Our three simple rules, posted in each of the areas used by the children, pretty much encompasses our philosophy: (1) you may not hurt yourself, (2) you may not hurt others, and (3) you may not hurt things, furniture, toys, etc.

Children who cannot be managed using these measures and are consistently presenting a discipline problem for the caregiver will be required to withdraw from care.

Substitute Caregivers

To help us through staff illnesses, holidays and training sessions, we may need to rely on substitute caregivers. A list of these caregivers is as follows:

_____ , _____
      (Name)   (Phone number)

_____ , _____

_____ , _____

This list is also posted on the Parent Information Board. We will do our best to help the children get to know our substitute caregivers before they are left in charge, and whenever possible, we will let parents know when a substitute will be used.

Releasing a Child From Care

Unless we are instructed in writing to do otherwise, The Magicland Daycare Center will only release a child to the following persons: (1) the child's parents, (2) when applicable the child's custodial parent, (3) the emergency contact person, and (4) any other guardian whom the parent, by way of a written authorization, allows us to release the child. We reserve the right to keep a child at the center if we are not completely certain about any person who has come to pick up the child. The parents will be contacted immediately if this happens.

Parent Participation

It is the law that parents are to have unrestricted visitation rights to any part of the center where the child is in care. We respect that right. Moreover, we encourage and welcome parent visits anytime. It is our belief that parent participation enhances the quality of care a child receives. Parents are free to join any of our activities.

To facilitate parent involvement, The Magicland Daycare Center offers the following: (1) a Parent Information Board for sharing thoughts and ideas, (2) monthly evening get-togethers, schedules and agendas are posted, and (3) a parent resource center in our reception area. Our Parent Advisory Council meets once a month (meetings are posted) and all parents are encouraged to attend.

Child Abuse

All caregivers are required by law to report any suspected cases of child abuse or neglect.

Parent Contract

During the pre-admission interview parents will be given a copy of our parent contract to review. If a parent chooses to place their child in the care of The Magicland Daycare Center, this form MUST be completed, dated and signed by both the parent and the director.

To help you formulate the purpose and philosophy portion of your policy statement, complete Worksheet #12.

2. Trial period

Your policy statement should include a trial period during which both you and the parent have the right to decide if the match is a favorable one. By favorable, I mean whether the child is able to get along with the other children in your care, whether your personality and the child's and the parent's are compatible, and whether you feel you can work with the family on an ongoing basis.

During the trial period you can contact a child's former caregiver(s) and question them about the care and the child. If you suspect trouble, you have every right to decline the provision of care. Parents should be made aware that this is part of your policy to do this sort of reference checking, even if it is only on certain occasions that you do so.

Sometimes you might find that, even after a successful initial interview and lengthy conversation over your policies and child-care contract, things do not turn out as you had hoped. Perhaps the child is adorable but the parent expects more than you can offer, or the parent is very accommodating but the child is ambivalent to any type of authority. If your policy statement clearly outlines your trial period policy, you have every right at the end of the period to explain your position to the parent and to decline the work.

As it would be unreasonable for you to terminate the care immediately (unless otherwise warranted), you should provide two or three weeks' notice of termination of care. Make sure you mention this in your policy statement at the end of the trial period section. You might also, at this point, offer to help parents locate more suitable care.

You should never feel guilty about declining to provide care because, in the end, it will ultimately prove better for all concerned.

3. Illness

The procedures you establish as a result of your consultation with the health nurse must be a part of your policy statement. For example, the list of symptoms for which you will call the parent to have them pick the child up should be noted, as should your procedures for isolating, discharging, and re-admitting an ill child.

You should also note that parents are required to complete a child medical report such as the one in Sample #16 in chapter 12, and that if a child is to receive medication of any kind, the parent must complete a written consent form for each and every medication.

4. Transportation and field trips

In your policy statement, let the parents know what kind of transportation is available and whether field trips are a part of your regular program. You should stipulate that before children can be transported anywhere, the parent will have to sign a transportation permission form (see Sample #8). When regular transportation is involved, a parent need only sign one form, which, as you will state in your policy statement, will be valid until terminated in writing by the parent. Each outing, on the other hand, will require a new form. You must convey in your policy that unless these forms are filled out, signed and dated by the parent, the child will not be allowed to take part in the outing.

Use your policy statement to outline the rules you expect the children to obey when being transported so that parents can teach them to the children.

5. Behavior management

In this section, you should include a statement of your philosophy concerning behavior management and a list of the rules

WORKSHEET #12
WRITING A PURPOSE AND PHILOSOPHY STATEMENT

Ask yourself these questions:

1. What is your purpose for starting a day care?

2. How do you plan to care for the children?

3. How will you help them to develop their social, intellectual, physical, and emotional skills?

4. What are your goals for the children?

Now look over the answers to your questions and write a paragraph or two working the main ideas into your purpose and philosophy statement:

and measures you will take to enforce them. Also make some statement about your policy regarding problem behavior and at what point you will request that a child be removed from care.

6. Supplies

If you are requesting that parents provide certain items such as diapers on an ongoing basis, you should put this in your policy statement so there is no mistake about who is responsible for what.

Parents of children that require diapers are required to provide sufficient supplies of diapers to allow the day care to conform to diapering regulations and the needs of the child. If a child runs out of diapers, the day care will purchase the required diapers and charge them to the parent. Parents of children who use cloth diapers are responsible for providing a diaper pail labelled with the child's name, removing the soiled diapers twice a week, and cleaning and disinfecting the pail before returning it. The Magicland Day Care does not provide laundry service for diapers.

To cover items that are used irregularly or on special occasions only, include a clause such as the one following:

Due to the constantly changing needs of the children in care, there may be times when parents will be requested to bring certain supplies to the day care. When these items are deemed necessary for the child's development or safety, the parent will be notified in writing of the exact items necessary, and will be given two weeks in which to furnish the items. If the parent fails to provide the items, the day care will make the necessary purchases and charge them to the parent.

7. Substitute caregivers

Outline in your statement under what circumstances you will be calling in a substitute caregiver (e.g., your illness, family emergency, etc.) and how much notice you will provide to the parent. You must also list the names and phone numbers of your substitutes.

8. Releasing the child from care

Inform parents of your terms and conditions for releasing a child from care and state that if you are uncertain about the person who comes to pick up the child, it is your policy to ask the person for identification and verify the release by contacting the parents. Mention that if you are still uncomfortable releasing the child, you will keep the child until the parents or emergency contact person arrives. For the most part, parents will respect and appreciate your position with regards to this policy.

9. Parent participation

As a child-care provider, it goes without saying that you welcome whatever assistance and guidance a parent is willing to offer. Some parents, however, are more comfortable in participating if you have a written policy explaining that you are most receptive to their involvement and active participation. In this section of your policy statement, state the parents' rights under the law, and then go on to mention what parental participation activities you offer beyond the legal minimum. Use language designed to encourage participation.

10. Emergencies

The following list will give you a general idea of the kind of information about emergency procedures that should be noted in your policy statement:

(a) The whereabouts of your emergency evacuation plans for every room. These should be conspicuous to both parents and staff.

(b) The frequency of practice drills for your evacuation, emergency, and disaster plans

(c) Your policy for contacting parents when a child is seriously ill or injured

(d) Your policy for administering first aid for minor injuries like cuts and bruises

Be sure to make it clear that each parent must complete and sign an emergency medical treatment form (see Sample #16) to allow you or any substitute caregiver to secure treatment for an ill or injured child.

11. Meals

In your policy statement, you'll want to let parents know which mealtime supplies or snacks, if any, they will be responsible for. Generally, this applies most often to the parents of infants who will need to supply formula and juice in bottles and to parents of children who require special diets. If a meal or snack cannot be easily prepared by you or your staff, make certain parents know they are to supply what you cannot. This should be noted both in your policy statement and in the child care agreement.

You will also want to state your usual mealtimes and your policy regarding foods served and/or permitted. You may want to forbid parents to send gum or candy with their child.

12. Child abuse

It is best that you let parents know in your policy statement that you must, by law, report any suspicions of neglect or of physical, sexual, or emotional abuse. To learn more about child abuse and recognizing the signs, please refer to chapter 17.

Peanut Butter and Honey Shaped Sandwiches

Butter

Bread slices

Peanut butter

Honey

- Butter bread.
- Spread peanut butter and honey over buttered bread and place bread together.
- Cut bread into shapes using cookie cutters.

8

FINDING CUSTOMERS

Marketing, by dictionary definition, is "the act or process of selling...in a market" (*Webster's Ninth New Collegiate Dictionary*). Sounds pretty simple, doesn't it? That is, unless the mere idea of selling sends a shock wave through your entire body and turns your brain to mush.

If you feel that way about marketing, cheer yourself with the thought that you are already are the road to marketing your business successfully. How can that be? you wonder. Okay, let's have a look.

The first step in any marketing program is to identify who your customers are, what type of product they want, and what they are willing to pay for that product. The assessment you did in chapter 2 to determine the need for child care should answer all these questions. So, you see, you are ready to move on to the next step in your marketing plan: reaching those customers and telling them you have what they want.

To do this, you will need to advertise using some or all of these methods:

    (a) Flyers

    (b) Bulletin boards

    (c) Newspapers and newsletters

    (d) The Yellow Pages

    (e) Associations

    (f) Word of mouth

Because your day care only needs to market within your community or perhaps on a city-wide scale, your advertising program will be small compared to businesses who market on a national or international scale. But like these bigger companies, your business must advertise effectively and within a budget. Weigh the benefits and costs of each type of advertising carefully before deciding which is appropriate for your business.

No matter what you decide, remember always that advertising is a form of communication. You are letting people know about the service you offer. There is no need for "hard sell" or extravagant promises. Of course, you should make sure that you represent yourself and your day care in the best light possible. You intend to provide high-quality day care, so say so. Always emphasize the benefits your day care offers that others, perhaps, don't. What makes yours unique?

For more on marketing and advertising see *Marketing Your Service Business* and *The Advertising Handbook,* two other titles in the Self-Counsel Series.

a. FLYERS

One of the most versatile types of advertising you can create is the simple flyer. A flyer can be folded in three to fit in an envelope, folded in two to slip through a mail slot, or not folded at all to be posted on a bulletin board or telephone pole. It can be elaborate and expensive, with photos and glossy paper, or fitted to the humblest budget using a photocopier, bulk paper, and clip art.

Your first flyer will be one announcing the opening of your day care. Just what should this announcement look like and what should it say? It can have a picture of your facility or drawings you have created to symbolize your service. It could be plain and practical or fancy and fanciful. The possibilities are endless; start-up funds, however, are not. More isn't necessarily better, either. You can create an ugly, ineffective flyer with expensive paper and colored inks just as easily as you can with cheaper supplies! For your first efforts, you are probably better off to use less-expensive materials and stick to one color for the paper and one color of ink.

Basically you want to tell your prospective customers six things: who, what, when, where, why, and how.

- Who you are (the name of your day care)
- What type of services you provide
- When you will be open (if not already)
- Where you are located
- Why they should use your services
- How they can contact you

Once you have included that basic information, you can add whatever you like to your flyer.

To give you some ideas on how to jazz up your announcement, collect some flyers or ads from other small businesses. Analyze them and decide what you like and don't like, what works and what doesn't. Then you can incorporate these elements into your flyer.

Sample #10 shows a typical flyer.

Who do you send your flyer to? If some respondents to your day-care needs assessment questionnaire provided you with their names, you already possess a list of people who are interested in knowing when you will open your day care. These are your potential customers and should be the recipients of the first notices you send out announcing the establishment of your facility. Your flyer should also be sent to the personnel departments of the businesses and facilities in your area. They should go to any other organizations you contacted during your assessment, including local schools. You might even want to send your flyer to the day care operators you talked to who have long waiting lists. Get your flyers into as many mail boxes in your community as possible.

b. BULLETIN BOARDS

Quick! How many places can you think of that have a bulletin board? Shopping centers, community centers, bowling alleys, laundromats, churches, and dozens of others. Write them down. Now, where are you going to post your flyers? Almost anywhere that people congregate, there are bulletin boards and a free opportunity to advertise.

Before you place your flyer on a bulletin board, check with the management to make sure this is okay. Some boards function on a permission basis only and it would be a waste for you to go to all the trouble of putting your flyer up only to have it come right back down. Others have size restrictions so your 8½ x 11 flyer may be too big. If so, go home, make up a card the appropriate size that still includes the most vital information (day care opening at —, ages 2 to 5, contact Mary Stewart, 555-1234), and post it up.

c. NEWSPAPER AND NEWSLETTER ADVERTISING

Newspapers are very expensive as a medium for advertising on an ongoing basis. This is one reason why you see few day cares advertising in the classified section of your paper.

When you first open your facility you will want to run an announcement of your new services in the paper. You have to get your name established. But once you are up and running, you shouldn't need to advertise in the newspaper except on special occasions or if your enrollment is down.

When you contact the newspaper about their rates, ask them about both their agate

NOW — QUALITY DAY CARE JUST MINUTES FROM YOUR DOOR

Magicland Day Care

11111 First Street

will be opening its doors on May 17

We are looking for children ages 2 to 5 for days of fun, learning, and loving care

The "Mom" at Magicland
Day Care is Mary Stewart

✔ Four years as a professional nurse

✔ Certificate in Child Nutrition

✔ Mother of two school-age children

✔ State licensed for day care

Our program
will include

★ crafts

★ games

★ songs

★ storytelling

★ weekly swim lessons at
   Grange Pool

Come to our Open House on May 10 to see how good day care can be!

Phone: 555-1234

line rate (the cost per line in a column) and their display rates. When you are announcing your business, a display ad will give you a more formal setting. The newspaper representative can help you design a good ad.

Community newsletters are an excellent and inexpensive advertising source. Since parents generally favor a facility close to their home, they will be very interested in learning about a new day care right in their neighborhood. A display ad in these publications will generally be a worthy investment and it will also keep your name before the public.

d. USING THE YELLOW PAGES

As entrepreneur Dan Kennedy says in his book *The Ultimate Marketing Plan*, "…the Yellow Pages are the most competitive, toughest advertising there is…" because your ad is surrounded by those of your competitors. In order to stand out from the pack, your ad has to offer your clients something different, something unique.

Why don't you, right now, turn to the day-care listing. If you live in a huge metropolitan area, you'll find not just one page of advertising, but five or ten. How on earth are you going to top all these ads?

Have a good look at them. Study them. Write down the ones that catch your attention and note what it was that drew you to the ad. Maybe it was a two-color ad, a cute animal character, a warm inviting look. Maybe it was the words, the way it was written that caught your attention. Write down everything you like about these ads and why you like them.

Now, what over and above all these wonderful advertising techniques would make your ad unique? How can you improve on these other advertisements to make your small piece of the page stand out?

Put yourself in your customer's place as you look over the Yellow Pages and ask yourself these questions:

(a) Why should I pick this day care over all the others?

(b) What does this one offer me that the others do not?

These are tough questions because you'll notice in the ads that every day care seems to have something special to offer, be it singing lessons, ballet dancing, or the warmth of a professional storyteller. Don't be intimidated. It is your turn to toot your own horn. Don't be shy. This is your business, your livelihood. Let the world know what's great about you and your service. Make them remember you.

The Yellow Pages representative can give you all the information you need to decide what size ad you should place. The representative can also help you lay out your ad and give you advice on how to make it more effective.

e. MARKETING BY ASSOCIATION

To help establish your day care you should join a few associations including both those in your community and national ones like the National Association for the Education of Young Children (NAEYC) or the Child Care Action Campaign (CCAC) in the United States, or the Canadian Child Care Federation (CCCF) in Canada. The addresses for these associations are in Appendix 2. They are but a few of the many organizations whose primary goal is to enhance and promote the quality of today's child care.

There are three major reasons for becoming associated with child-care organizations:

(a) Your membership in this type of association assures parents of your commitment to your facility and the children therein.

(b) Through the various newsletters produced by these associations, you will receive up-to-date information about the world of child care that you can then pass on to your customers.

(c) You can keep abreast of seminars and other educational materials that will help you in providing optimum care.

Becoming a member of local respected organizations promotes an image within your community that you are committed to providing a better way of life for children both inside and outside of your day care. Never underestimate the value of building a good image within your community. Your association connections also make for great references in your Yellow Pages advertisement.

f. WORD-OF-MOUTH ADVERTISING

Walt Disney once said, "Do what you do so well that people can't resist telling others about you." This is what you should aim for. If you have a genuine love for the children you care for, parents will notice. They will also notice the cleanliness of your facility and the excitement the children have at some activity they did that day. If your day care is clean and you are eager to help the children and to work one-on-one with parents, you will have no trouble finding and keeping customers. The reason: word-of-mouth advertising.

When a customer is satisfied, he or she feels comfortable recommending you to friends and coworkers. It is this recommendation that will help to keep your day care operating at full capacity. When you can operate on this scale, you will find you have enough funds to upgrade your equipment, your supplies, and your program. This is when you can offer children the best-quality care.

Word-of-mouth advertising is free and it is the best advertising you will find. If you have any doubt as to its value, consider this: Joe Girard, the author of *How to Sell Anything to Anybody*, wrote his Rule 52 after he realized that the median number of persons who attended a wedding or funeral was 52. Each of your customers, he concluded, has the capacity to refer you and your business to 52 persons. Even if that is only half true, a 26-person-per-customer reference base is considerable by any standards. With that in mind, remember that a dissatisfied customer also has the potential to turn away many customers from your services. Provide the best care you can and people will enthusiastically tell others about it.

You can, in fact, ask your customers for referrals. Don't be shy. Ask them to give your cards or flyers to their friends and coworkers. If they love your services, they will gladly pass out your literature. Ask them if they know of anyone who is having problems with their current child-care arrangements or who is just returning to work. If they are reluctant to give you actual names and addresses, give them as much information about your facility as you can and ask them to pass it on.

g. YOUR LOGO

Whatever type of advertising you choose, creating and using a particular style and logo on all your advertising and written materials will give your day care a professional image and promote recognition. Spell out your day care's name in big block letters with a couple of toys sitting on or around the words, or use flowers, fuzzy animals, or rainbows. Do you want to be seen as warm and friendly or bold and adventurous? Is your style soothing, pastel, and full of butterflies, or exciting, fire-engine red, and carried on the backs of charging ponies? Is your day care conservative? Avant-garde? Educational? You could even use something as simple as your day care's name simply spelled out in large, fancy type.

The key to making your design work as a logo is to use the same design all the time, in every possible way, making all your marketing tools easily recognizable and memorable, like a trademark. Put it on a front-yard sign, if your zoning allows. Paint it on your car and on the aprons the kids use while doing crafts. Put it on your stationery, your forms, your business cards, your flyers. Print it on the kids' "report cards." Use it in ads. You are creating an image for your day care and ensuring that it is noticed and remembered.

h. PUBLICITY

Loosely described, publicity is getting public attention for your day care from media such as radio and newspaper, and getting it for free.

1. Radio bulletin boards

Many radio stations have on-air community bulletin boards where they will play your public announcement over the airwaves for free. Give your local station(s) a call to find out exactly how you get your message on the air and then follow through. Your copy will have to be short, so write tight and snappy. For example —

> Parents in the Sunnyvale community will be pleased to know that a new day care for children 2 to 5 is opening on the corner of Spruce and Grove. For more information on Magicland Day Care's hours and programs, call Mary Stewart at 555-1234.

The radio station may edit your announcement to fit their time allotments, but you can rest assured they won't leave out the important stuff.

2. The news release

Getting your facility opening into the pages of the local newspaper will take a little more creativity. Call the paper and ask which editor or reporter would be most interested in receiving your announcement, then send that person a news release.

A news release is a short, written statement that makes the opening of your day care sound like news. This is the key to getting your news release printed — make it sound exciting, newsy, something that everyone in your community should read about (see Sample #11).

Always remember when writing your press release that you are writing a news story, not an advertisement. In theory, the press release is your opportunity to tell the media all about your business. But in practice, it is not actually written from your personal point of view. Instead, it is prepared by you as if you were a newspaper reporter interviewing yourself. For this reason, you must always refer to yourself in the third person — "he" or "she" or "Jane Smith." The personal pronouns, "I," "me," and "mine," should never appear unless you are quoting someone and the quote appears in quotation marks.

A press release must be written in journalistic style, concentrating on the facts and not speculations or opinions. "Jane Smith says her day care provides services no others do" is a fact — you, the writer, are not saying that the day care provides unique services but that Jane Smith says so. This is an important distinction, even if, in reality, you are Jane Smith. But if you write "Magicland Day Care is a wonderful place for children," without attributing it as a quote by someone, this is only the writer's opinion, and the reader's instinctive reaction is skepticism. If you want to include this kind of opinion statement, use a quote, even if you attribute it to yourself. Of course, if you can get quotes from others (such as the

* NEWS RELEASE *

May 5, 1993   Contact: Mary Stewart
FOR IMMEDIATE RELEASE   555-1234

PARENTS' DEMANDS HEARD BY LOCAL BUSINESS

Long waiting lists in the city's day cares have prompted the opening of a new facility, the Magicland Day Care. Located at 11111 First Street, this newly renovated in-home day care is scheduled to open its doors to a waiting public on May 17.

With an average wait of six to eight months for a day-care space, the need for more quality day care is desperate.

"Parents are forced to line up toddler day care as soon as a child is born," says Joan Small, a pediatric nurse.

Magicland's owner, Mary Stewart, became aware of this problem when her own first child was born.

"I talked to other mothers in the maternity ward and one of their major concerns about having a baby was how they were going to find good day care when they wanted to go back to work."

Stewart, who was interested in starting a business, says that day care seemed to provide both a promising business opportunity and a chance to serve the community.

"Parents should be able to go off to work with confidence that their children are being well looked after. Children should be happy and fulfilled in their care situation. By starting Magicland, I can help meet these needs and run a successful business as well."

To better acquaint the community and the surrounding business district with this quality day care, Magicland Day Care will be hosting an Open House on Friday, May 10 from 11 a.m. until 8 p.m. Members of the public, no matter where they live in Yourtown, are also welcome. Children and parents are encouraged to explore the facilities at their leisure and to partake in a variety of scheduled activities.

For more information on the Magicland Day Care, this event, or for a private viewing, please contact Mary Stewart at 555-1234 between the hours of 8 a.m. and 6 p.m.

- END -

one from Joan Small in Sample #11) and get the speaker's permission to use the quote, you are lending more interest and credence to your story.

Start your news release with an attention-grabbing headline. Where will you find such a headline? Try your assessment. Was there something you found in your assessment that totally shocked you or made you realize that starting your center was the absolutely right thing to do? Or, if your program is going to feature something unique, try that out as a headline: Luxury Day Care To Offer Riding Lessons, Ballet. Another possibility is to tie your day care to an event: Magicland Open House To Feature Clown, Balloons, Games. Whatever you decide on, make sure it sounds like something you'd pick up and read if you were the reader.

Immediately following your headline is your first paragraph containing the five W's — who, what, where, when, why. It's important to get the most important facts into the first paragraph because this is the way news stories are written. That way, if the story is too long, the editor can simply cut from the bottom without losing the most important part of the story.

Your final lines should let the public know who to contact for more information.

When you lay out your news release, do so on your letterhead, leaving a 1" (2.5 cm) border on all sides. Type the final copy double–spaced and try to keep it to one page. At the end, use one of the following symbols, - END -, - 30 -, or * * *.

Have a few copies done up at your local printers then send them out a few weeks in advance of your opening to give the paper sufficient lead time to cover your story. Send the release to newspapers, community newsletters, city magazines, and local television stations. Address the mailing to the appropriate person at each office, making sure you have the name spelled correctly.

3. Keep it up

Even after your day care is open and doing good business, it is a good idea to keep your business's name before the public by using press releases and radio announcements. Again, you can link your publicity to events to make it newsy. "Local day care hosts parenting seminar" or "Children's author to read at Magicland" are genuine events that local media are likely to pick up on. The more people hear of you, the more likely you are to have customers beating down your door — a pleasant situation for any business.

For more information on publicity, see *Getting Publicity*, another title in the Self-Counsel Series.

i. REFERRAL AGENCIES

The increase in the number of new resource and referral agencies across North America signals the coming together of a highly fragmented and diverse child-care system. These agencies offer caregivers, early childhood educators, family service bureaus, consumers, and other persons and organizations concerned with child care an opportunity to join forces to share a variety of information and resources.

These systems can be as complex as the National Association of Child Care Resource and Referral Agencies (NACCRRA), which provides information from across the country, to the individual referral agencies such as the Children's Council of Red Deer Society, whose primary concern is the dissemination of child-care information within their own communities.

It would be in the best interests of your business to look into all the aspects of these referral agencies and inquire about either becoming a member or applying to have your facility listed in their data banks. This is very important for a number of reasons. When parents contact a referral agency looking for a licensed facility in their area, you want to make sure you are on that list.

Your being associated or recommended in this fashion assures parents that they have placed their child in a quality program. It also tells your parents and community that you are serious about the care you provide.

To find out about local, state or provincial, and national referral agencies and associations, contact the offices listed in Appendix 2.

j. THE MARKETING ACTIVITY SHEET

Using a marketing activity sheet such as the one provided in Worksheet #13 will help you plan and work through your advertising and promotional campaign. Start to fill it out now and continue to enter the dates of your various activities as you begin and complete them.

WORKSHEET #13
MARKETING ACTIVITY SHEET

Activity	Date started	Date completed
New facility announcement flyers		
Flyers written		
Flyers printed		
Sent to:		
names from assessment		
personnel department of local businesses		
health facilities		
parent advisory council		
elementary school		
organizations contacted during assessment		
mail boxes throughout community		
Yellow Pages ad		
Contact with rep		
Ad composed		
Associations		
Research		
Write for info		
National joined		
Local joined		
Newspaper advertising		
Research		
Contact with rep		
Ad composed		

Activity	Date started	Date completed
Newsletter advertising		
Research		
Contact with rep		
Ad composed		
Bulletin board placements		
Research		
Ad composed		
Ad placed:		
1.		
2.		
3.		
4.		
5.		
News releases		
Release written		
Release printed		
Sent to:		
radio stations		
newspapers		
community newsletters		
TV stations		
Referral agencies		
Research		
Write for info		
National joined		
State/Provincial joined		
Local joined		

I Spy

Can be played with two or more children.

Object of the game: To guess from clues what the other player "spies."

How to play: One child looks around the room and picks an object. The others have to guess what it is. The child gives clues one at a time by saying "I spy with my little eye something that is red," and so on. The other children each get a turn to try and guess what the object is. If no one gets the right answer, the spy can keep giving clues until someone guesses. The child who guesses correctly gets to be the next spy.

9

THE NEW CUSTOMER

The happy moment arrives when the first parent calls to inquire about your services. Your marketing is beginning to pay off. You can hardly contain your enthusiasm, which is good as long as you are prepared to handle the call and don't come off sounding like a bumbling fool. As the saying goes, you only get one chance to make a first impression, and your day-care business, like any other business, is dependent on your creating an image customers can trust.

a. HANDLING THOSE TELEPHONE CALLS

The first thing you should do is set up an area by your telephone where you keep plenty of paper, writing instruments, and a list of questions that will guide you through the initial telephone contact with ease. You might even want to have pre-printed notepads or sheets that list the required questions. Then all you have to do is fill in the information in the appropriate place as the caller answers your questions.

Make it a point to teach family members the proper way to answer the telephone and how to take a message so you can return the call.

Some of the information you'll want to get from the parent right away includes the following:

(a) Parent's name

(b) Parent's home and work number

(c) Child's name and age

(d) Hours of care required

(e) Approximately when the child would begin at your day care

While you are gathering the information you require, parents will also be asking you about your rates, hours, vacancies, policies, and references. This is the time to make your policies known to prevent misunderstandings and unpleasantness later on.

Although you will know much of this information off the top of your head, there will be times when some of this information will slip your mind. To the rescue: an information sheet tacked up right by the telephone (see Sample #12).

This sheet should contain all the data you need to know at a glance: your rates for the different age groups, what vacancies you have, how many children you are currently caring for (including your own), their ages, directions via the major road arteries to your location, special services you provide, a quick note about yourself, the day care, and your qualifications, and lastly, the names and telephone numbers of at least two references. You should also list the name and number of your local child-care referral agency, and, perhaps, the names and numbers of one or two other caregivers in your area.

If it becomes apparent that you cannot offer assistance to the parent because of incompatible time requirements, unavailability of space, or some other reason, tell the caller you don't think the arrangement will work out and why, and thank him or her for calling. At this point, you might want to refer the parent to other caregivers in your area who may be able to help, or you can offer the telephone number of your local child-care resource and referral agency. It is much easier to refuse at the

TELEPHONE INFORMATION SHEET

RATES:		Full Time	Part Time	Casual (per hour)
	Infants:	$400	$23	$3
	Toddlers:	$375	$20	$3
	Preschoolers:	$350	$20	$3
	School-age:	n/a	n/a	$3
	Special needs:	$500	$25	$5
	After School:	n/a	n/a	$3
	Two Children Families	$700	$30	$4
	Three Children Families	$800	$35	$4
	Overtime:	$1 per minute the parent is late		
	Overnight:	$25 per evening per child		
	Long Day Rate: (10 ½ - 12 hours)	$460	$25	n/a

VACANCIES:	Full Time	Part Time	Casual
Infants:		1 afternoon only	
Toddlers:	1	1	
Preschoolers:	None	None	
School-age:	None	None	
Special needs:	None	None	

NUMBER OF CHILDREN IN CARE: 4

	Ages:	11 months,	23 months,	3 years,	4 years
Infants:		1, morning only			
Toddlers:			1, full time		
Preschoolers:				2, full time	
School-age: None					
Special needs: None					

LOCATION: Via <u>Queenston Expressway to Oak Road:</u>

turn left at Elm Street; drive 3 blocks; corner lot with a big sign — can't miss it.

               Via <u>Stoney Brook Drive to Elm Street:</u>

go south 2 blocks; corner lot with a big sign — can't miss it.

SPECIAL SERVICES: <u>Volunteer reader — children participate in "story time" at the library. One field trip per month. We accept children overnight and on the occasional weekend.</u>

CAREGIVER QUALIFICATIONS:

<u>1-year Early Childhood Education Certificate Program;</u>
<u>Current first aid and CPR certificate</u>

STAFF QUALIFICATIONS:

Substitute: <u>Mary Williams, retired schoolteacher. First aid and CPR.</u>
Volunteer: <u>Joyce Caron: part-time librarian. Reads to the children.</u>

REFERENCES:

Name: <u>Harriet Smith</u>   Number: <u>555-6796</u>
Name: <u>Janice Walker</u>   Number: <u>555-4328</u>
Name: <u>Patricia Benson</u> Number: <u>555-9625</u>

LOCAL REFERRAL AGENCY: <u>Childcare Unlimited. 555-9292</u>

LOCAL DAY CARES:

<u>Woodland Elementary School (before and after school program run by YWCA),   555-7926.</u>
<u>Rainbow Riders Day Care, 555-4377.</u>

onset, over the telephone, than to go through the trial period and realize you and the parent or child are simply not compatible with each other.

If, on the other hand, your services and the needs of the parent seem to be a good match, the next step is to set up a personal interview for the parent to visit your facility and meet with you. If at all possible, it is best if you interview the parent alone without their child(ren), possibly after hours or on the weekend. This will enable you to talk with the parent without interruption.

It is not a good idea to accept a child into your care without first interviewing the parent in person and discussing your house rules and policies. Don't be tempted to agree immediately to take the child just because the parent is in a bind — you could be regretting it for months.

There may be times when you are simply too busy to answer the phone, times such as lunch or nap period. A good answering machine with a message conveying the reason for your temporary unavailability is a good investment. Remember, however, that parents of the children in your care may also be trying to get through. Therefore, you should make limited use of answering machines and let parents know when the machine will be turned on so they are not calling over and over again, needlessly worrying about why you are not answering their calls.

b. THE PERSONAL INTERVIEW

Congratulations! You've made it through the important first step and have set up a personal interview. Getting through this interview successfully will be a matter of how well you are prepared. The interview is an opportunity for you and the parent to get to know each other and discuss your views on childrearing. You will also discuss your policies and the paperwork required.

The interview should run as smoothly as possible and be a relaxing time for both you and the parent, so go over your interview procedure and set out an interview schedule. Make notes on an index card to prompt you during the interview or practice your interview with a friend or spouse. For example, when the parent arrives, a personal chat over a cup of coffee would be a nice introduction. You could then introduce your information package (see section **c.** below), discuss its details, and respond to any questions the parent may have.

During this time, ask the parent if the child has been in care before and, if so, the type of care, the name of the facility or provider, and why the child is leaving the care. This will give you some indication as to exactly what type of care the parent is looking for and whether you feel you will be able to provide that care. It will also alert you to potential problems. If the parent is reluctant to tell you who cared for the child before or why he or she is no longer there, your warning bells should start ringing. You may be in danger of inheriting a real problem, so be careful.

Once this portion of your interview is complete, you will want to take the parent on a tour of your home or facility, pausing to answer questions or to give the parent an opportunity to make some mental observations. The parent should see all the areas where care will be provided, namely the sleeping area, eating area, bathroom facility, the indoor play area, and the outdoor play area.

Your facility should speak highly for itself, so make sure it is clean and tidy before the visit. Your program will be judged by the parent's perception of the comfort and contentment of the children in your care, if he or she visits during working hours.

The next step would be to return to your sitting area to talk over any questions or concerns the parent may have. This would be a good time to give the parent a copy of your child-care agreement for them to look over and fill out if they decide to place their child in your care.

Not every parent you interview will hire you. An informed parent will visit a number of caregivers or facilities before deciding which one will best suit the family's needs. It is a personal decision that does not in any way reflect on you or the type of care you provide.

If you do come to an understanding, you might suggest that the parent and child(ren) visit your home a few times before the care is scheduled to begin to help the family adjust to the new arrangements. With each visit, the parent could leave the child alone in your care for longer periods of time. This way, when the time comes for Mom or Dad to head off to work, everyone will feel more relaxed and comfortable.

c. THE INFORMATION PACKAGE

Should the parent express a desire to sign the child(ren) into your care, be certain they fill out all the forms in your information package. These forms will include the following:

(a) Rate sheet with general outline of basic fees, overtime fees, absentee fees, holiday pay, method and frequency of payment and annual increases (see Sample #7).

(b) Hours sheet including times during which the day care is open, the days care will be provided, and a statement regarding holiday closures

(c) Substitute care statement including under what circumstances you will bring in substitute care and the names of the people who will provide the care

(d) Policy statement (as discussed in chapter 7 and shown in Sample #9) with a general overview of your child-care program, trial period, discipline policies, safety procedures, meals and snacks, the ill child, toilet training, parent participation, trial period, suspicion of child abuse, and your policy regarding the release of a child to anyone other than the parent or guardian

(e) Sample program outline including daily and weekly activity schedules, group size, and outings

(f) Child-care agreement which the parent signs to agree to all of the above (see Sample #13)

(g) Medical/emergency form detailing the child's medical health, medication, allergies, and a release to seek medical attention in the case of an emergency (see Sample #16)

Note that each regional child-care authority has its own regulations as to exactly what information is to be given to parents during a pre–admission interview. Consult the office in your area for more information.

CHILD CARE AGREEMENT

The following agreement is made between:
Magicland Day Care
1111 First Street
Yourtown, Ont. K0B 1C0
555-1234

and

Parent's Name(s): <u>John Black</u>
Address: <u>2222 Second Street</u>
Telephone Number: <u>Home: 555-4321 Work: 555-8765</u>

For the provision of child care for:

Child's Name: <u>Kim Black</u>

Child's Name:

the terms of our agreement are as follows:

Hours of care: <u>7:30 (a.m.) to 4:30 (p.m.)</u>

Days of care: <u>Weekdays</u>

Fee for care: <u>$550,</u> is due and payable not later than the beginning of the last day of care for each month.

Fee is to be paid <u>monthly,</u> by <u>check or cash.</u>

This fee is payable whether the child does or does not attend care on the days as agreed upon above.

Late or overtime fees of <u>$1.00 per minute</u> apply when the child is not picked up by 15 minutes after the scheduled pick-up time as noted above, and will be due and payable upon the arrival of the parent or guardian to pick up the child.

The items listed as follows will be supplied by the parents: <u>diapers, formula, special diet foods, weather-appropriate change of clothing</u>

Breakfast, lunch, and snacks will be provided by the day care.

For the termination of care, both parties agree to submit to the other: <u>three weeks written notice</u>.

Written notification will be given by the center for: <u>increases in child care fees, unscheduled center closings</u>.

Written notification will be given by the parent for: <u>vacation periods and/or extended absentee days</u>.

Magicland Day Care is not obligated to hold open a child's child-care spot after 20 absentee days by the child.

Mary Stewart
Caregiver's signature

John Black
Parent's signature

September 6, 1993
Date

Pizza Dreams

Bread slices

Butter

Ketchup

Grated cheddar or mozzarella cheese

Toppings: green pepper, salami, ham, mushrooms, pineapple, tomatoes

- Lightly butter bread and spread with ketchup.
- Put on desired toppings. Cover with cheese.
- Toast in a toaster oven or a conventional oven at 375°F (191°C) until cheese is melted and bread browns lightly.

10
PROGRAM PLANNING

After all the terms and conditions of your policy statement have been discussed, after your rates, hours, and annual increases have been reviewed, parents are going to ask you one more question: What exactly is my child going to be doing at your day care?

Good program planning involves an understanding of child development and age-appropriate activities and learning materials, the security of predictable events, and a curriculum that meets the needs of the children in the program. It promotes development in children by attending to their physical, emotional, social, and intellectual needs. It is the framework under which children flourish. Providing this is a tall order, which is why most states and provinces demand that day-care operators have formal early childhood education training.

So, before you venture into program planning, you require an understanding of the components that make a program successful.

a. WHAT CHILDREN NEED

The only difference between adults and children is age. Think about it. Our needs are the same — we yearn to feel loved, understood, and a part of the world. We must have our physical needs met through nourishment, rest, and exercise. Social creatures, we long for friendships, loving relationships, and caring. We need to learn, to experience the world around us, and to understand and accept ourselves as part of the wonder and challenge of it all. These needs are, indeed, universal.

In order for a child to develop his or her full potential, these needs must be addressed. Therefore, your program should include nourishing meals, rest periods, and individual play. It must also involve group activities to enhance social skills, outdoor play to develop large muscles, play and learning materials that help the child discover creative and intellectual abilities, and a caregiver who shares all of the child's experiences, good or bad, so that he or she can learn to trust and feel secure.

To learn more about children's needs and their learning development, visit your library for some reading on the subject or take a course at your local college.

The Early Childhood Program Guide, a document published by the Newfoundland Department of Education, uses the terms *long times* and *brief times* to help caregivers understand a child's need for uninterrupted periods of time where he or she can complete activities that require more time and attention — for example, artwork, block building, or puzzles and games. By allowing for long times of one-half hour to an hour or more, you will foster longer attention spans, something children need if they're going to succeed at school. A child's self-confidence grows as he or she is able to complete more demanding tasks.

A caregiver who sets up art activities and then tells the children to put everything away 10 minutes later is actually doing the children more harm than if the children had not been allowed to do art at all. What the children experience instead is frustration and dissatisfaction at not being allowed to finish.

Long times can be incorporated into your program by using larger slots of time. Plan these activities for long times:

- Free play or activity centers can be long times that give children the freedom to choose their own activities, to make independent choices.

- Active play allows children to develop their large muscles and to make use of the energy we all know children have.

- Small-group activities, where the group is limited to eight or fewer children, provide an opportunity for the children to interact closely with peers and caregivers, enhancing social skills. Activities could include stories or games.

- Nap times or rest periods are also included in the long times. All children, whether they nap or not, need a time during the day when they can rest. Generally, the children should be allowed to sleep for at least one and a half hours. For those who are not nappers, they should be given books, puzzles, or some other form of quiet activity to do, but this should only be provided after the child has had an opportunity for solitary rest of at least one-half hour.

Brief times, on the other hand, allow you to schedule activities such as clean-up, snack and lunch periods, and transition times when children are dressing to go outside, using the washroom, or waking up from nap time. Some, like bathroom time, will only take 10 minutes, but it is important to put them in your schedule along with the longer activities.

b. CREATING A DAILY SCHEDULE

When creating your schedule, begin by sketching in general times for standard activities such as meals, clean-ups, diaper changes, and naps. These are the "bare bones" of your program. Your licensing requirements and your good sense will help guide you here.

With your basic routines in place, you can begin to fill in the other activities. When planning these activities, vary active times with quiet times, lessening the stress and fatigue common with long stimulation periods. Try to allow enough time for each activity so that the children are not rushed through it, but are given sufficient time to learn from what they are doing, to induce longer attention spans, and to foster a feeling of accomplishment and self-worth. Keep transition times brief, helping the children as they go along.

When scheduling arts and crafts, allow time for setup and cleanup and keep in mind that projects that take longer than five minutes to set up or clean up may prove hectic for both you and the children.

Sample #14 shows what a typical daily schedule might look like.

Finally, while your program should guide you, flexibility is important. If the children want to stand at the window watching the snow flakes fall rather than listening to a story, follow their lead. Learn from their behavior and, if need be, adjust your routines and schedules. For example, if you find the children are boisterous and playful after lunch even though they already played outside during the morning, change your outdoor time to after lunch.

MAGICLAND DAY CARE

DAILY SCHEDULE

Time (Approximate)	Activity
6:45 - 7:45	Arrival. Free play in centers. Older children may assist with breakfast preparation and table setting.
7:45 - 8:00	Cleanup and hand washing.
8:00 - 8:30	Breakfast.
8:30 - 8:45	Cleanup, wash, and brush teeth, diaper change.
8:45 - 9:30	Art, craft, manipulative activities (beads, blocks, play dough, puzzles).
9:30 - 9:45	Cleanup.
9:45 - 10:45	Group activities (dancing, music, puppet play, stories, chatting sessions, or circle games).
10:45 - 11:00	Snack.
11:00 - 12:00	Outdoor play (indoor in inclement weather) to exercise large muscles.
12:00 - 12:15	Change from outdoor clothing, wash up for lunch.
12:15 - 12:45	Lunch.
12:45 - 1:00	Cleanup, quiet play.
1:00 - 2:00	Rest and nap time. (babies nap until 2:30)
2:00 - 2:15	Wake up, cuddle and toilet time; diaper change.
2:15 - 3:15	Free play at centers.
3:15 - 3:30	Cleanup, wash up for snack.
3:30 - 3:45	Snack.
3:45 - 4:30	Outdoor play.
4:30 - 5:00	Group activities.
5:00 - 5:30	Free play in quiet areas (blocks, beads, puzzles, play dough), departure.

c. CHOOSING ACTIVITIES FOR A CHILD'S DEVELOPMENT

When I began in child care, I played with the children, helped them to development, and gave them a lot of love. Not very sophisticated, but the children were happy, the parents were happy, and I thought I was doing the best possible for the children.

The truth is, I wish I had known then what I know now. My choice of activities may have been fine, but I knew very little about child development, and even less about child-appropriate toys, equipment, and learning materials. I can recall going into a teachers' store at a local mall, looking at the many supplies, then leaving empty-handed because I had no idea of what I should buy for the kids. Many of the items even frightened me when I realized that before I could allow the children to use these toys, I first had to understand how they worked and of what practical use they could possibly be.

In retrospect, I realize now what a difference some of those toys would have made. Visiting my children at school has taught me how the games and the materials they use are very important tools. Instead of drilling on the addition and multiplication tables, the children unconsciously memorize and visualize them while they play. The paper *Guidelines for appropriate curriculum content and assessment in programs serving children ages 3 through 8*, which is put out by the National Association for the Education of Young Children and the National Association of Early Childhood Specialists in States Departments of Education, says that "Learning occurs in children's minds as a result of an interaction — an interaction between thought and experience, an interaction with a physical object, or an interaction between a child and an adult, or between children and their peers.*" This

is what you must build on in planning fun yet educational activities for the children in your care.

Naturally, the activities you choose will be dependent on the ages and development of the children. For instance, infants who are just beginning to crawl are not ready to play the active games the toddler group enjoys, games like Duck Duck Goose and Ring–Around–the–Rosy, any more than toddlers are ready for thinking games like I Spy and Twenty Questions, which the preschool group relishes. This may appear a simplification of child development, but it does illustrate distinct differences in the stages of physical, social, intellectual, and emotional growth.

Let's take a closer look at these four areas of growth.

Physical growth consists of the changes that take place in the child's body as he or she grows. As the child gets older, he or she develops both gross motor skills (the ability to use the large muscles for activities such as climbing, running, and riding a tricycle) and fine motor skills (the ability to control smaller muscles for cutting, coloring, and manipulating small objects like buttons).

Intellectual growth is the increase in mental capacity to do things such as learn and reason. Almost from birth, Baby Jane learns that when she cries, Mommy will come. After a few months, Baby Joey learns from grabbing for his rattle that those funny-looking things he has been staring at and sucking on for a couple of months now, his hands, actually have a purpose.

Social growth is the change in the ability to relate to and interact with others. A child's social growth takes him or her from an infant's total self-involvement through to enjoyment of team games as a six-year-old.

---

*This paper is must reading for anyone interested in planning a preschool program. You can obtain a copy by writing to the National Association for the Education of Young Children, 1834 Connecticut Avenue N.W., Washington, DC 20009-5786.

Emotional growth is the development of and recognition of feelings such as love, fear, sadness, anger, and happiness. While very young children may experience these feelings, they also need to learn what they are feeling and how to express these feelings.

Activities that foster continuous development in these areas need not be elaborate. In fact, free play, the least structured activity imaginable, encourages children to try new toys, build a taller tower, act out family roles, cooperate with their friends, and learn that if they want the other kid's toy, they have to wait their turn. The caregiver's job at free time is to simply set up certain materials like paints, intercede when disputes arise, encourage one more block (but not doing it herself), demonstrate an alternate method when a child becomes frustrated, or just be there to praise efforts.

The caregiver who takes in several children of differing ages faces a problem in planning activities, as he or she must plan the activity to challenge every child without frustrating or boring any. Understanding child development and knowing what to expect of each child will certainly make this task easier.

For example, Pam is caring for a 12-month-old, two 2-year-olds, a 4-year-old and a 5-year-old. In planning her art activity, Pam wants to give the children an opportunity to develop their fine motor skills by cutting, pasting, and coloring a collage. The two oldest children do not require much assistance, so, except for the odd request for help, she is free to concentrate her help on the 2-year-olds who are only now beginning to use scissors. The baby is seated in the high chair beside her, enabling her to talk and coo with him at the same time as she is working with the other children. She has given him a magazine to look and tug at. Before too long, it becomes apparent that one of the 2-year-olds is content to flip through the magazine and comment on the pictures. Pam does not push her to do the art work, but rather respects her show of independence. She also knows that as the child looks through the magazine, she is developing her language skills as she chats constantly about what she sees.

Table #1 is a child development chart for you to refer to when planning your activities. The chart outlines what an average child is like at a certain age. As you know, all children develop at different rates and variations in development are likely. However, if you notice a child is lagging behind in a certain area of his or her development, it is best you notify the child's parents and suggest that perhaps they might want to schedule a visit with the child's pediatrician to discuss the matter.

Table #2 will give you some ideas about appropriate activities for the different age groups.

d. WEEKLY ACTIVITY CHART

While your daily schedule outlines what your general schedule will be every day, a weekly activity chart provides a more detailed picture of your activities on a particular day or through a specific week. For example, if your daily schedule says "Arts and crafts" between 2:30 and 3:30 daily, your weekly schedule will list exactly which arts and crafts activities you have planned for that period every day of that week.

A weekly activity chart serves the following purposes:

(a) It allows you to plan far enough ahead to pick up the materials, books, and so on that you will need for the week.

(b) It gives you a chance to discuss the weeks' happenings with the children and to ask for their thoughts and ideas, penciling them in as you go.

TABLE #1
CHILD DEVELOPMENT CHART

AGE (approximate)	ABILITIES	INTELLECT	SOCIAL	ACTIVITIES
1 - 3 months	Can follow many persons and objects with eyes Begins to reach with hands Can lift head for a few minutes Stares at objects	Laughs and coos Listens to voices Enjoys the sound of music	Recognizes parents Smiles at those he/she knows, especially parents	Singing, nursery rhymes Mobile close so that baby can swing at it
3 - 6 months	Explores hands and feet Puts objects in mouth Sits with support Rolls on own Stands when pulled into position Loves to bounce	Imitates sounds Transfers objects from one hand to another	Smiles a lot Laughs and giggles Recognizes voices, particularly those of parents	Peek-a-boo Singing and music Rattles and soft toys the baby can feel and mouth Finger plays
6 - 12 months	Sits without support Creeps and crawls Pulls self into standing position Feeds self simple foods like crackers Walks around furniture with help from adult	Speaks and understands common words Puts objects into and out of pails, cartons Can locate hidden objects	Knows own name May be shy with strangers Loves to socialize	Simple roll and catch games Patta-cake Enjoys blocks, stuffed animals, nesting toys, board books, magazines
12 - 18 months	Feeds self Walks well Begins stair climbing Runs stiffly Begins to use fine motor skills; scribbling, working with smaller objects Throws objects, tries to catch	Identifies body parts Understands possession — "mine" Has a 10-15 word vocabulary Can recognize objects in books	Develops friendships Interested in world around them, dogs, peers	Large-piece puzzles Coloring with fat or big crayons or markers Water and sand play Use of large cardboard box to play in Enjoys music, stories, working with objects, playing ball
18 - 24 months	Runs well Stacks 6-8 blocks Folds paper Tries to dress self	Carries out simple directions Uses 2-3 word sentences Beginning to use pretend play	Likes to play alone even when other children are around Independent, resists parents' interference	Stringing large beads and spools Enjoys play dough, painting, plastic farm animals, free play at centers

TABLE #1 — Continued

AGE (approximate)	ABILITIES	INTELLECT	SOCIAL	ACTIVITIES
2 - 3 years	Rides a tricycle Uses alternating feet up and down stairs Copies circles Helps with dressing	Language develops rapidly Uses 3 - 4 word sentences Vocabulary about 50 words Short attention span — around 10 minutes	Plays simple games with other children Imitates adult behavior (playing house, etc.) Likes to help with chores	Puzzles, painting, play dough, picture book stories, music, finger painting Likes pounding boards with hammers, riding tricycles, playing dress-up
3 - 5 years	Learns to hop, skip, and jump Enjoys playing catch Can use scissors Rides a two-wheeler with training wheels	Longer attention span Asks many questions Understands some rights and wrongs Play becomes more dramatic	Likes to talk a lot Enjoys friends Learning to take turns Hates to lose May have an imaginary friend	Simple card and board games, puzzles Enjoys music, may want own tapes or records Likes to work with wood, sanding and cutting Enjoys water and sand play Uses bats and balls, roller skates, musical instruments, bean toss Dolls are important Likes more complex books
5 - 8 years	Physical abilities continue to improve Coordination increases — balancing, skating, skipping	Child's intellect develops substantially Learns to read, write, and understand addition and subtraction Vocabulary increases dramatically Enjoys a challenge but also likes to see the final product of a project Uses words to express feelings and emotions	Plays cooperatively Likes team activities Becoming more aware of the world around Considers feelings of others May have a best friend Needs time for independent play or to be alone	Tougher puzzles Enjoys arts and crafts of all kinds, chapter books, tools, and wood Still likes water and sand play Interested in cash registers, typewriters, and computers Has a vast array of interests

TABLE #2
ACTIVITY IDEA CHARTS

INFANTS
0 - 18 months

Physical

Does not require structured activities. Enjoys games like Patta-Cake and Peek-A-Boo, hiding the object, throwing things for you to pick up. Fine motor skill activities include: grasping for objects — you could play a game where you move the object and make the baby reach for or grab at it. Needs room to roll, crawl, climb. Enjoys sitting on your lap and being pulled to a standing position. Older children like to push and pull things — provide for this with little shopping carts, wagons.

Intellectual

Loves to touch and be touched. Stroke the baby with different materials like a feather, velvet, a soft brush, satin, cowhide. Give the child plenty of opportunities to feel and manipulate various objects, like rattles of different shapes and textures, teething rings, a wet face cloth, Freezies. Provide for dramatic play with dolls, cars and trucks, dress up clothes, stuffed animals. Needs to interact with toys. Free play is essential.

Social

Loves the sound of voices, singing, and music. Talk face to face with the baby. Read to him. Tickle him, play with his hands and feet. He needs to be around people.

Emotional

Needs a lot of cuddling, cooing, tickling, being fussed with. Praise is essential in all areas of development from self-feeding to throwing a ball. Staff participation is crucial to his well-being.

Language

Talk constantly to and with the baby. Point to objects like ears, eyes, feet, hands and say the corresponding words. Repeat this activity often. Ask the older baby to point as you repeat the words. Pointing games are also great with word picture books, using pictures of cats, dogs, Mom, Dad, boy, girl, etc. Read to the baby often.

TODDLER
18 months - 36 months

Physical

Requires lots of free play. Teacher required to initiate activities. Games like hopscotch, soccer, catch, and tag are popular. Drawing with colored chalk on the sidewalk or the side of the building is fun and washes away with water or rain. Cut straws into little pieces and let the children string necklaces and bracelets. Coloring over objects placed

112

TABLE #2 — Continued

	under a piece of paper makes for interesting art work (i.e. keys, leaves, money, paper clips). Dancing to simple tunes doing movements that involve clapping hands over the head, turning around, touching their toes, jumping up straight.
Intellectual	Small group activities are best. Needs you to help with taking turns and to initiate some activities. Games that involve the senses like catching snowflakes and watching them melt, blindfold games of guessing the smell of certain foods, the feel of different objects, the sound of different noises. Make scrapbooks using magazines to sort different objects like cars, toys, food, houses. Dramatic play like grocery store, doctor, hospital, restaurant, beauty parlor, farmer. Pictures using different materials like soap drawings on colored construction paper, paintings sprinkled with salt, macaroni, flowers. Bubble play, doll bathing, and toy washing are good water games.
Social	Dancing with various materials like scarves, streamers, batons. Interactive games like tunnel chasing, ball rolling, hide-n-seek. Bean bag toss using an old box with 6" diameter holes cut in it. Circle time with child-told stories about "Where I Live" and "In My Neighbourhood."
Emotional	Needs a lot of praise and encouragement. Display artwork and other collectables where the parents can see, but low enough where the children can demonstrate their work.
Language	Read to the children every day. Simple word and picture books are best. Play telephone. Toddlers need a talkative adult around to stimulate conversation and foster language development. Ask the child lots of open-ended questions like "What color chalk would you like to use today?" "What might happen if...?" Provide activities that compare items, like "What makes the apple and the orange different?" etc. Use circle time to talk about grandparents, birds, dreams, fairy tales, favorite stuffed toys, and so on.
PRESCHOOL 3 - 5 years	
Physical	Lots of fun ideas here — T-ball, throwing and catching games, leap frog, tag, obstacle course with jumping, balancing, running, crawling, and climbing activities. Excercise games like Simon Says, jumping on one foot, pretending to be a tree in the wind. Arts and crafts like finger painting, making objects with pipe cleaners, making

TABLE #2 — Continued

mobiles with items found on a nature walk by using a stick or large twig, string and leaves, pine cones, nut shells, etc. Secret messages or pictures made with soap on white paper can be uncovered when rubbed with a pencil. Ring-toss game can be made from cardboard rings the children cut out and paint. Buttons, bottle caps, small rocks make excellent tossing items.

Intellectual

Activities that involve pattern-making are important, arranging different objects according to size, color, texture, make. Nature walks are great for this age group. Look for signs of spring, crawly bugs, different leaves, birds, butterflies. Look at the different seeds in various fruits. Plant seeds in different containers. Designing table settings and practicing setting the table are good for building math concepts. Cover a child's eyes with a scarf and let him taste different foods, feel different objects. Sort the items in the dress-up box before laundering. Play memory games like putting a few items on the table, letting the children observe them, and then covering them up and asking the children to name all of the items that are there. Use several foam cups and hide one item under one cup. Shift the cups around and have them guess which cup contains the item.

Social

Dramatic play is important. Initiate games like playing dentist, doctor, school. Let the children make many of their own props. Puppet shows are popular and easy to make. Discuss issues like what makes people sad, taking care of yourself, keeping yourself safe, and so on during circle time. Singing and dancing also enhance social skills. Let the children dress up in funny costumes before they dance, find a funny song to sing.

Emotional

Again, a child needs a lot of praise and individual attention. Show an interest in their thoughts — let them initiate activities. Read books about feelings, sharing, being a friend.

Language

Conversation plays a big part in a child's language development. Provide plenty of opportunities for the children to express their feelings and thoughts. Ask open-ended questions often, like "Do you think these two kinds of shoes are good for the cold weather?" or "Will it work if...?" Read to the children every day. Let them put on puppet shows. Make story books using pictures from magazines. Let the children tell stories during circle time. Play an imagination game where you ask the children to imagine they are different animals, foods, people. Ask what it would be like to be these things. How would they survive? What would they eat?

(c) It gives parents a chance to see what their child will be doing for the next week and provides them with an opportunity to discuss it with you if they have any concerns or ideas.

(d) It provides you with a record of what activities you have covered and, if you make notes, can let you know which activities the children enjoyed the most and would like to do again.

You could choose a "theme" for the week and build some activities around that theme. For example, you might choose a "spring" theme, and have the children do coloring and pasting of flowers and bunnies one day, read them a story about spring the next day, sing some spring songs another day, and so on. Sample #15 is a typical weekly activity chart.

When it comes to planning a week's worth of activities, the *Mister Rogers' Plan and Play Book*, which outlines the show's 600-plus episodes, is full of ideas. The producers of the "Mister Rogers' Neighbourhood" have initiated a child-care providers' program called *Neighbors in Child Care*. Along with the Mister Rogers' book, providers receive *Neighbors in Child Care*, the quarterly newsletter outlining the weekly themes and the individual shows that will be aired. The program also has a training course for providers who are interested in learning how to use the book and how to follow up viewing of the television program with related activities.

Even if television is not part of your activities, the book and its over 400 pages of songs, art and craft projects, and themes that deal with such issues as personal grooming, feelings, mistakes, growing up, and so on, would be a good addition to your resource library. The book itself costs around $10. To receive more information on this program, contact:

Family Communications Inc.
4802 Fifth Avenue
Pittsburgh, PA 15213

WEEKLY ACTIVITY CHART
This week's theme is <u>the jungle</u>

Day	Art/craft	Group Indoor	Group Outdoor	Freeplay Items
Mon	Popsicle stick build-ings	Story: "The Baby Ele-phant"	Game: Cross the River	Plastic jun-gle animals
Tues	Cut and paste: paper plate mon-keys	Song/game: "Zebra, gnu, I love you"	Game: Open, Open Wider	
Wed	Painting: rainbow ze-bras	Puppet story: "The Lion and the Jackal"	Game/exer-cise: Jungle animals do	
Thur	Egg carton alligators	Movie: "The Jungle Book"	Game: Who's the Hippo?	Play dough cutters in jungle ani-mals
Fri	Coloring: jungle plants	Story: "Crocodile Tears"	Outing: Walk to park	Felt jungle animals

Red Light, Green Light

For groups of four or more.

Object of the game: To be the first one to the other side without getting caught while moving.

How to play: All the children except the one who is IT line up against a wall. The person who is IT stands against the opposite wall or on a rope marking the finish line. IT, with eyes closed, turns away from the others and yells "Green light!" This is a signal for the other children to come forward. When IT yells "Red light!" and turns around, they must stop and stand perfectly still. If IT sees anyone moving after he or she turns around, that person is caught and sent back to the beginning. The first one to the finish line gets to be IT.

11

PLAY

Play is very hard work! It takes concentration, energy, time, skills, and enthusiasm. And just look at what a child can do by the time he or she is ready for school: walk, talk, and eat without help; run, jump and use the bathroom; count, recognize numbers, and imitate animal noises; cut, paste, and paint; understand about sharing and not hurting others. That is quite an accomplishment. And to think the child learns all that from playing.

A child learns more in the first five years of life than in any other five-year span of life. A quality child-care play program gives a child the freedom and opportunity to reach his or her full potential. It provides the equipment with which to learn, an environment that stimulates curiosity, and the nurturing that bonds it all together.

A perfect play environment is put together with the right equipment and lots of imagination — you provide the equipment and the children will provide the imagination! The best play equipment is often the good old standbys like blocks, stacking things, cars, dolls, balls, crayons, puzzles, books, play dough, paints, and push toys. These are the items that children will return to again and again and at various ages. Your major concern is making certain there are enough of these toys for the number and ages of the children you plan to care for. As we mentioned in chapter 4, however, these items do not necessarily have to be purchased new. Next-to-new toys can be found at flea markets, garage sales, and thrift and secondhand stores at a fraction of the cost.

a. WHAT ARE LEARNING CENTERS?

On any given day, when I ask my son what he did in school that afternoon, he's likely to tell me, "Oh, we just had 'centers.'" When I ask him what he did during "centers," he says, "We played, Mom." I guess that's today's language for we figured out how to build a boat out of play dough so that it would float on water, (water center), or we mixed sand in the paint then brushed different colors onto the paper to see how it would look (art center). Fun stuff, all right.

But by manipulating the play dough, they were learning about space and weight. They also worked — or played rather — in different groups, learning to cooperate and learning from each other. That is what learning centers are all about.

A learning center is a small area of activity devoted to a specific type of play: art, crafts, math, water, books, etc. You can easily set up different learning centers in your home on trays, little tables, or, like the book center, on a shelf. Simply arrange at the center the materials you offer and let the children play as they will. You can provide guidance or suggestions for things to do with the material, but ultimately the choice is theirs. Regardless of what little Janey does with the materials, she is learning something about either the material or herself and her abilities to manipulate and work with the material. At the very least, if Paul and Janey worked on making a snake train with the play dough, they have learned to work cooperatively, and that in itself, is a worthwhile achievement.

The list of different learning centers you can create is virtually endless. Here are just a few possibilities:

- housekeeping center
- art center
- construction center
- quiet center
- library or book center
- sand and water center
- music center

Now, let's take a closer look at some learning centers and what materials they require. Always keep in mind that not all materials may be suitable for all age groups. For safety reasons, young children should not be playing with nuts and bolts and other small items, or with sharp objects like saws. Match the materials to the levels of the children using them.

b. HOUSEKEEPING CENTER

This is one learning center that will get a lot of use. The housekeeping area is a stage for much dramatic play, from playing Mommy, Daddy, and baby, to dressing up like Aunt Lucy; from cooking and cleaning to shopping and playing restaurant. The center does not have to be elaborate. If you cannot afford to purchase plastic or wooden children's kitchen furniture, you can create some using sturdy cardboard boxes. Kitchen supplies could come from used egg cartons, food boxes, margarine containers, old measuring cups, and plastic utensils. Dress-up clothing, well, you remember from your childhood — anything will do. Listed below are some items you'll need and others you might want to throw in just for fun.

Need:

- stove
- sink
- cupboards
- small tables and chairs
- pots
- pans
- utensils
- cups
- plates
- bowls
- ironing board
- plastic iron
- broom
- dustpan
- doll crib or cradle
- dolls
- plastic food items
- puppets
- old boxes
- empty egg cartons
- play phone
- cardboard boxes of all shapes and sizes
- play dough
- cookie cutters
- rolling pin
- oven mitts

Optional:

- food coupons
- magazines
- play money

- cash register
- newspapers
- menus
- pencils
- note pad
- chef hats
- place mats

Dress-up clothes:

- shirts
- skirts
- dresses
- pants
- sweaters
- blouses
- hats
- scarves
- ties
- purses
- shoes
- socks
- coats
- jackets
- shawls
- full-length mylar mirror

c. ART CENTER

The art center is a world in itself. So much imagination, so much color, so much creativity — so much mess! We'll disregard the latter as one of life's little pitfalls, after all, what is art if it is not messy?

Children love to experiment with color, texture, and paper. Aside from unleashing hidden Rembrandts, art benefits children in many ways. It utilizes the muscles in the hands (small motor skills), which helps ready them for the tasks of writing and ma-

nipulating small objects like buttons and zippers. It also teaches them to see beauty in life, in art, in themselves.

As you prepare to stock your art area or cupboard, there are two items you should particularly avoid:

(a) *Coloring books.* These are often frustrating for younger children who have trouble coloring within the lines. Besides, you want to draw on a child's own creativity rather than on someone else's

(b) *Markers, paints, and glues that are not marked as non-toxic.* There are many art supplies on the market containing toxins that can be absorbed into the skin or inhaled into the lungs. These supplies are not recommended for use by children.

Need:

- paint smocks or aprons
- tempera paints
- brushes
- safety scissors
- glue sticks
- white glue (water-based)
- crayons
- markers
- construction paper
- playdough
- chalkboard
- chalk
- brush
- paint easels
- pie tins for mixing paint
- glue
- scotch tape
- stapler

- yarn
- string
- beads
- sponges
- popsicle sticks
- tongue depressors
- pencils

Optional:

- crepe paper
- brown wrapping paper
- hole puncher
- tracing molds
- paper bags
- corkboard and pins for displaying art

Art is a very private form of self-expression. Each child sees the world in a different way and is unique in that view. You should respect a child's art for what it is, for the valiant effort they put forth in producing the piece. When a child presents you with a finished work, ask him or her to tell you about it. Comment on the color, the use of different materials. Avoid asking the child what the picture is if you are uncertain. The child's commentary will suffice. Try not to compare the work the children do or give suggestions on how to make it better; if the child is satisfied, that's what counts.

d. CONSTRUCTION CENTER

This center requires a bit of floor space as the children are involved in more active play using blocks of various shapes and sizes, farm sets, cars and trucks, construction materials, and roadway equipment.

Blocks are one of the best toys for this center. You can build skyscrapers with them, or line them all up for a roadway. You can build a fence to corral the horses, or you can stack them evenly in rows to make towns.

What are the children learning? Plenty. It takes coordination to build a skyscraper. It takes counting and visual cognition to line up a bunch of houses the same height. A roadway takes precision in lining blocks up perfectly, as does building a fence. Through it all, it takes imagination, which the children demonstrate over and over again with the number of things they construct.

Integrate the blocks with other types of materials such as foam rubber pieces, sandpaper, airplanes, cars, trucks, play people, string, and longer pieces of lumber. You'll be amazed at how many engineers of all sorts you have in your group. Lego, Tinkertoys, and other more sophisticated building toys are great for the older children.

Boxes are a source of inspiration for children and they are handy toy makers for providers as well. Play or club houses, even a post office, can emerge from a giant appliance box and can be decorated inside and out. Tunnels are another idea, as are puppet theaters and doll houses. Boxes can be decorated by the children and used to store their private items like mittens, hats, scarves, and so on. The possibilities are endless.

Need:

- assortment of blocks
- Lego
- foam rubber scraps
- nuts and bolts
- tools
- corks
- cardboard boxes
- lumber scraps
- farm and zoo sets
- airplanes

- cars
- trucks
- dump trucks to hold blocks
- little people

Optional:

- hammer
- nails
- sandpaper
- saws
- paint
- block attachments to make steering wheels and road signs
- Tinkertoys

e. QUIET CENTER

Children sometimes need a place where they can get away from the hustle and bustle of activity and play quietly by themselves. One such place would be the quiet center.

Here the child can work on a puzzle, string beads, stack toys, thread cardboard pictures, use a flannel board with shapes and numbers, or any number of activities that one can play by oneself. Such quiet activities exercise the fine motor skills. They also teach concepts of sequences (a math-readiness skill) by allowing children to string beads in a certain repeated order, recognize and use variations in shapes, letters, and numbers.

Need:

- wooden puzzles
- regular puzzles
- beads of various shapes, sizes, and colors
- string
- nesting boxes
- flannel board and accessories
- card games

- sorting objects such as buttons, shells, and rocks

Optional:

- picture dominoes
- nest of rings

f. BOOK CENTER

The library or book center is another quiet place for children to take a break from the noise and excitement of the general group. All children love books. They like to flip through the pages and look at the pictures. What better way to learn stories and nursery rhymes and poems and to learn words — all kinds of words from big serious words to silly, fun words.

Have a great variety of books. Nursery rhyme books are great, but children find other books like number and counting books, animal books, and picture books just as fascinating. The more you can offer children, the more you will pique their interest in reading.

If you are not sure which books to buy, talk to the children's librarian at your local library. She can tell you what sort of books children prefer and what age group is best suited to which type of books. Your local and/or national library association can also give you information on purchasing children's books. To that end, Health and Welfare Canada, Child Care Program, has a booklet titled, *Good Books for a Good Start*, which breaks the reading experience into age groups and describes the different types of books that are best suited to these groups. There is even a segment on "Using Children's Books in Child Care" and "Books, Parents and Child Care." You can obtain a copy of this booklet by writing to:

Child Care Program
Health and Welfare Canada
Sixth Floor, Brooke Claxton Building
Tunney's Pasture
Ottawa, Ontario
K1A 1B5

Many books now come with an audiocassette of the story. If you are so inclined, you might consider setting up a tape recorder in your book center to allow the children to listen to their favorite books, which they will do over and over again.

Need:

- board books
- nursery rhymes
- poetry books
- alphabet books
- counting books
- picture books
- fairy tale books
- animal stories
- books with no text

Optional:

- hardcover as opposed to softcover

g. SAND AND WATER CENTER

Sand and water play is both fun and educational for the children. They can learn to pour and to build. They can learn which objects float and which sink. They can play for hours on end using sponges, strainers, basters, and shovels. Think of the science they are learning. To top it off, sand and water are fun things to touch.

Plastic water and sand tables can be purchased through toy and equipment suppliers. If you do not have the funds to purchase these, the children can still engage in water play in the sink, in a washtub on the table, or in the bathtub (under close supervision).

Need:

- plastic bibs or aprons
- sand table
- sand (non toxic)
- buckets

- shovels
- plastic containers of all shapes and sizes
- sieves
- strainers
- funnels
- water table or wash tub
- plastic measuring containers
- things that float
- things that sink

Optional:

- cars
- trucks
- tractors
- farm animals
- wire whisks
- egg beaters
- basters
- dolls

h. MUSIC CENTER

I can't think of any child who doesn't enjoy music. Perhaps they enjoy it because it is the one time they are allowed to make noise! Ouch! But there is so much more to music than noise. There is dancing and singing to engage in, records and tapes to listen to, and instruments to play. And there is the sheer enjoyment of it all.

If that weren't enough, music is also a very educational tool. The repetition of songs helps to build memory and vocabulary, while at the same time, as children struggle to learn the words, they sharpen their listening skills. Group singing enhances social skills while dance improves coordination, as does instrument playing. Above all else, music is portable. You can sing in the car, along the walk to the park, while the children are washing up for meals and snacks. You can sing anytime, anywhere.

For children, you don't necessarily need to buy real instruments. They can have just as much fun with homemade versions that are a lot cheaper and easier to replace. In addition, you and the children can enjoy making many of your "instruments" using simple items from around the house.

Need:

- drums — coffee cans with plastic lids, ice cream buckets, plastic or metal containers

- drum sticks — wooden spoons, doweling of different sizes, paint stirs, broom handles

- cymbals — pot lids, pie tins

- maracas — yogurt containers filled with gravel, beans, rice, or sand

- sand blocks — blocks of wood with sandpaper glued on to them

- tambourine — pie tin with bottle caps, paper plates with jingle bells attached

- rhythm sticks — broom sticks, doweling, wooden spoons

Optional:

- Real instruments purchased new or used

- record player

- records

- tape player

- tapes

- song books

i. OTHER CENTERS

You could classify these as shoe-box centers, as the supplies can be kept in a box and brought out when needed.

1. Math center

- Counting items such as bread tags, buttons, small blocks, beads, shells, rocks

- Equipment for measuring such as rulers, measuring tape, measuring spoons, and cups

- Plastic numbers, number games, flash cards, play money, cash register, calendar, bingo, clocks, timers, etc.

2. Science center

- Pets, small toy greenhouses, measuring cups, rocks, magnifying glass, bug catchers, plants, shells, magnets, prisms, compass, items that involve the senses; sight, taste, smell, hearing, and touch

3. Camping center

- Backpacks, sleeping bags, tents or large pieces of material or blankets that can be used to cover areas, old pots and pans, grill, canteen, binoculars, cooler

4. Infant center

- Rattles, squeeze toys, mobiles, board and cloth books, nesting and stacking toys, stuffed animals, soft balls, washable dolls

j. OUTDOOR PLAY

A little boy gives a squeal of delight. There is glee in his face and a twinkle in his eye. Confidence radiates from his three-year-old body. "I did it. I did it!" he shouts, running as fast as he can to the back of the slide, eager to climb the ladder one more time, all by himself, then push his limber body down the plastic half-tunnel.

There is a phenomenon at work here. It's called self-confidence. As the boy learned to correctly position his feet and his legs to absorb the shock of his slide to the ground and finally succeeded at climbing the height of the slide and positioning his body without falling and without assistance, he experienced the pride and pleasure of mastering a physical skill. He learned that he could challenge himself to do something he couldn't do before, and then work at it and practice until he *could* do it.

The outdoor play area is the place where children can run, climb, and be free. As their muscles develop and their abilities to perform grow almost daily, so, too, does their inner self. It is the confidence within that enables them to climb one rung higher than the day before, to run a bit faster, to reach out and make one more friend, to share of themselves when a friend is having trouble. This is why outdoor play is so very important.

For an outdoor play center to challenge a child, it must be generously equipped and well designed. Read as much as you can about outdoor play center planning before purchasing any equipment as it is more complex than at first appears. There are numerous books and research papers written on the topic and you can apply their theories to your play center.

Space is, of course, essential. Many licensing boards have rules about the area and the design and type of equipment necessary to facilitate a certain amount of children. For the home day care, space may prove to be a problem. If you don't have a large backyard, it would be a good idea to scout your neighborhood for parks and open fields where the children can run and play ball. These facilities, combined with whatever outdoor space you do have at home, should prove sufficient as long as you have a good supply of outdoor toys and a few major pieces of equipment, like those included in the list below. Obviously, you choice of equipment is going to be limited by your budget and space available.

Need:

- a lot of space
- good fence with child-proof latches
- sunny and shady areas
- grass (soft surface)

- cement or asphalt (hard surface)
- wading pool
- picnic table
- wagon
- push and pull toys
- balls, various shapes and materials
- jump ropes
- baseball
- bat
- T-ball
- nature tools (magnifying glass, bug catchers, shovels)
- blocks, big and small
- cars
- trucks
- garden hose
- boxes
- pipes etc. for children to climb through

Optional:

- jungle gym or adventure center
- pet center
- benches
- old tires
- punching bags
- tetherball
- climbing apparatus
- slide
- tricycles
- peddle vehicles
- balance beam
- sand box
- sand (non toxic)
- sand toys

Outdoor activities need not be restricted to the use of the equipment listed above. When the weather is good you can do a great many things outdoors including story time, painting, nature activities, building snow castles, music, tea parties (snack time), and eating lunch outside.

On the other hand, bad-weather days are no excuse for omitting physical activity from the program. There are numerous games that can be played indoors, and by moving the odd piece of furniture, you can set up an area in your home where the children can romp around, do somersaults, dance, and climb in and out or on and off of big boxes. You could cover up the coffee table and use it as a tunnel. Or, you could lay a skipping rope across the floor for the children to pretend they are tightrope walking. How about making a hopscotch on a plastic sheet and securing it with velcro? The variety of activities is as endless as your imagination.

k. STAYING ORGANIZED AND HAVING FUN

For everything to run smoothly as you and the children go through your rounds of activities, you need to have some organization and cleanup routines as well. Staying organized and cleaning up can be part of the fun, if you handle it right. You should not do all or even most of the work — the children will learn little from that. You simply need to motivate and direct the activity.

Make a game of cleaning up: "Let's see if Joe and Sue can get the blocks picked up and put away before Mary and I can clean up the kitchen." And you whistle or sing while you work. That always makes cleanup seem much less of a chore. A few minutes before cleanup time, let the children know they should finish what they are doing because cleanup time is in five minutes.

Organize your toy and center areas so that children have easy access to them. Store play materials in an orderly fashion so the children can find them, play with them, and then return them to their proper spot when they are finished. Toy boxes are not recommended as the clutter inside discourages imagination and the toys may be ignored. Also, lids on toy boxes have been known to slam down on little heads and fingers causing injuries.

Instead, arrange to have low shelves built into your play area or purchase small bookshelves. Toys set up on shelves facilitate both curiosity and easy cleanup. Brick and board shelves work well for this purpose. Bookshelves can also be used as room dividers. Old dressers or storage cabinets make excellent places to store toys and equipment. At day's end, they can be closed up and tidy.

Crayons, markets, sorting toys, and the like can be kept on the shelves in see-through plastic containers (store-bought versions, or milk and pop crates). These allow the children to see what is inside the container without pulling each box off the shelf and possibly spilling the contents.

Do not put all the toys out at one time. Several toys placed in a box can be rotated with the shelf toys on a regular basis or when the children become bored with their current assortment. Rotating toys in this fashion keeps them alive and interesting.

l. TOY LIBRARIES

Toy libraries are a wonderful resource. They offer, on loan, a variety of toys and equipment. The loan period varies between two and three weeks and although there is generally no charge to borrow the toys, there is an annual membership fee. You will often find that toy libraries are a service of a local family resource center, community organization, child care registry, or home day care association. To find out more about the toy library in your area, contact your local child care resource and referral agency.

m. GAMES

Your play heaven would not be complete without a few games to play during group time and outside time. I'm sure each of us has some favorite game we relish from our own childhood days and it seems that most of the games being enjoyed by children today are ones that have been handed down from one generation to the next. Somehow childhood never really changes.

If you play competitive games where a particular child "wins" or "loses," make sure you choose a variety of games to allow each child a turn at winning or losing. If, for example, one child is a good runner, and you frequently play games that involve running, chasing, and catching, not only is that child going to get a superior attitude, but the other children are going to lose enthusiasm for games where they feel the winner is already decided. To avoid this, add variety with memory games, guessing games, thinking games, or non-competitive games.

As you will have noticed by this time, descriptions of games start off some of the chapters in this book. These include:

- Duck, Duck, Goose (chapter 1)
- Ring-Around-The-Rosy (chapter 3)
- The Farmer in the Dell (chapter 5)
- Skipping Songs (chapter 7)
- I Spy (chapter 9)
- Red Light, Green Light (chapter 11)
- Musical Chairs (chapter 13)
- Simon Says (chapter 15)
- London Bridge (chapter 17)
- What Time Is It, Mr. Wolf? (chapter 19)

Here are three books about children's games that I highly recommend:

- Brandreth, Gyles. *The World's Best Indoor Games*. New York: Pantheon, 1981.
- Diagram Group. *The Way to Play*. London: Paddington Press, 1975.
- Evans, Patricia. *Rimbles: A Book of Children's Classic Games, Rhymes, Songs, and Sayings*. New York: Doubleday, 1961.

Sandwich Rolls

Bread slices

Butter

Cream cheese

Ham, chicken, or turkey slices

- Remove crusts from bread slices.
- Butter lightly.
- Spread cream cheese on bread, then cover with a slice of luncheon meat.
- Roll up like sausage rolls.
- Can eat as is or can be cut into decorative bite-size pieces.

12
HEALTH AND SAFETY

One of the saddest, most heart-wrenching things to look at is the face of a sick or hurt child. Those solemn eyes and those pouty lips have a silent cry that is hard to ignore. And you often think to yourself, If I could only make it all better. But you can't. Disease, colds, flu, viruses, little mishaps — they are an inescapable part of life. Children, who have not yet built up immunities and who are so much more active yet awkward than adults, are susceptible to a point where it seems they are always sick or hurt.

What you can do is work diligently to make their environment — your day care — as healthy and safe as you can. You can't prevent Annie's sniffles or Alfie's tumble, but you can prevent Annie's sniffles from turning into an epidemic among the other children and you can prevent Alfie's tumble from being a tragedy.

a. WHY CAREGIVERS HAVE TO WORRY ABOUT "LITTLE" ILLNESSES

It is a fact that children in day care suffer from illness more than children cared for by their own parents. Why? Because whenever you have a number of children coming together from different environments and sharing the same toys, floor space, air space, and equipment, you are producing a breeding ground for every type of virus that these children, through their individual families, encounter. The results can be an epidemic of sorts.

How does this happen? It happens because these viruses live in every drool, runny nose, sneeze, and cough. And since children play so closely with each other, they share these bugs without realizing it. The toys are sneezed on, picked up and mouthed; noses are wiped on hands and shirt sleeves, the children touch each other and again, the hands contact the mouth; Annie coughs with her face unprotected, spewing droplets into the air; Jessica inhales these droplets, unaware that she will also share her buddy's cold. And so it goes.

This is where you come in. If the natural order of things were to continue, there would never be a healthy child in your day care. For that matter, you and your family would also be constantly ill. To stop the spread of these germs and keep illnesses from infecting everyone, you must establish a clear set of health procedures and practices for your day care.

b. PREVENTING THE SPREAD OF GERMS

The best defense is a good offense: no truer words were ever spoken, especially when it relates to the war against infection and disease. Fighting the invisible enemy will take some strategic planning. Following are some rules you might want to incorporate into your battle plan.

1. Hand washing

Hand washing is the number one weapon in germ fighting. Imagine all the germs a person picks up over the course of a day. Now imagine how quickly these germs can be washed away. In the minute it takes to turn on the tap, lather up, scrub, and rinse, all those cold- and flu-causing nasties are flushed down the drain forever. Until your hands touch something else that is infected. The moral of the story: you must establish clear guidelines about frequent and regular hand washing in your center. With practice, these guidelines will become habit and, in this case, forming habits is good. Following are some general rules to follow.

(a) Hands must be washed —

   (i) before any food is handled,

   (ii) after food is handled,

   (iii) after using the toilet,

   (iv) after each and every diaper change, and

   (v) after each nose wipe, sneeze catch, or cough cover. Whenever you assist with nose wiping, etc., you should place the tissue directly into the trash container and then wash your hands. The children should do the same. Tissue sharing is a no-no.

(b) Place a poster showing good hand-washing techniques above all sinks where the children can see and refer to them often. Sometimes a gentle reminder is all it takes.

(c) Establish regular hand-washing routines with the children, like lining up to wash before and after meals, having their hands checked after they leave the bathroom, and going straight to the bathroom after they use a tissue.

(d) Use only paper towels; cloth towels collect germs.

(e) Premoistened "handy wipes" should not be used in place of soap and water as they do not clean properly.

2. Diapering

Some infections such as viral enteritis, shigella, and hepatitis A are transmitted via bowel movements, most commonly when something like food or a rattle touched by contaminated hands is put in the mouth. Diapering and the way in which it is performed has a lot to do with the transmission of these diseases. Clearly established diapering guidelines are necessary to reduce the rate of such occurrences. These guidelines should include the following:

(a) Set up the diaper-changing area away from the food-preparation and consumption area. The changing area should be close to a deep sink to allow you easy access to hand washing after diapering.

(b) Wear rubber gloves when changing diapers and thoroughly wash your hands after each diaper change.

(c) Ensure that the changing surface is made of a non-porous material or covered with a heavy vinyl that is free of cuts or holes. This area should be sanitized with a bleach solution (one part bleach to nine parts water) after each diaper change.

(d) Dispose of or store soiled diapers properly in a tight container, away from the mainstream of activity and certainly out of the reach of the children.

3. After using the toilet

Children should be taught to wipe, flush, and then wash their hands thoroughly. Stepstools placed at the sink make this easier for a child. Potty chairs should be emptied immediately after being used and should be cleaned with a bleach solution. All facilities should be cleaned with a bleach solution at the day's end.

4. Food preparation

Anyone responsible for food preparation must wash their hands thoroughly before food is handled. Children who assist in the food preparation must also wash their hands thoroughly. Food preparation services must be kept clean and dry and must be separate from diaper-changing and playing areas. These surfaces, particularly cutting boards and dishes, must be free of cuts, cracks, and chips, which are a refuge for germs.

Dishes washed in a dishwasher should have 1 tbsp. of bleach added to the rinse cycle and left to air day. Dishes washed by hand should be rinsed in a solution of bleach water (1 tbsp. bleach to 2 gallons of water) and left to air dry.

Store perishable food items at 40°F (4°C) or below and tightly sealed. Food should never be left to thaw at room temperature, but should be left in the refrigerator to thaw. You can also use a microwave oven to thaw the food. Leftover food should be refrigerated or frozen for future use right after the meal is complete. These foods should not be left out for any length of time.

5. Other helpful hints

Below are a few more ideas you might consider implementing as part of the overall health practices of your center or home. These ideas are relatively simple and not very time-consuming.

(a) Open windows daily if only for a few minutes. Fresh air is good at inhibiting the spread of germs. It is also important for children to play outside whenever possible.

(b) Keep all toys, furniture, and equipment clean and sanitized with the bleach solution. Crib rails, high chairs, and strollers also need to be cleaned regularly — at minimum once a week.

(c) Keep children separated when sleeping. Place cots or beds far enough apart so an adult can safely walk between them. This is important for safety reasons also. When space is not available between beds, have children sleep in alternating positions (i.e. head, feet, head, feet).

(d) All sheets, linens, and dress-up clothing should be laundered once a week.

(e) Make yours a smoke-free home.

(f) Keep each child's toothbrush and comb apart from the others. Each child should have his or her own face cloth. All personal items should be marked and stored separately, including coats, hats, etc.

(g) Sanitize all garbage and diaper containers weekly.

(h) Make the bleach solution daily, otherwise the bleach may evaporate and the solution would then be ineffective.

c. IMMUNIZATION

Immunization is the best defense any child has against some of the most deadly childhood diseases such as diphtheria, whooping cough, tetanus, measles, mumps, rubella, polio, and meningitis. It is your job to check the immunization record of every child who is seeking care. The National Association for the Education of Young Children recommends that programs should exclude children who are not properly immunized. For the protection of the other children in your care, your family, and yourself, unless a child has documented proof of his or her immunization record, or until a doctor's note is secured in its place, you have to say no.

d. RECOGNIZING COMMUNICABLE DISEASES

Every morning when a child arrives for care, the first thing you should do is check the child's health. During this assessment you note if a child is well or if he or she is exhibiting signs that the child is too ill to be in care that day. In order to make an accurate assessment, you have to recognize the common signs of many childhood diseases. The health of your entire day care depends on this ability.

With the help of the public health nurse and a pediatrician or physician who has agreed to act as a referral for your center, you can learn to recognize a skin rash, understand the danger signals of a fever, vomiting, or diarrhea, and to listen to the parent's concern when you discuss the child's wellness in the morning. Learning to recognize communicable diseases gives you leverage in the battle against disease in that you can isolate a child with an illness early enough to stop the spread of the disease.

The list that follows outlines some important symptoms you should be aware of:

- Fever of 101°F (38.5°C).
- Diarrhea
- Severe coughing where the child gets red or blue in the face or makes a high-pitched whooping sound after a cough
- Difficult or rapid breathing
- Conjunctivitis (irritation and redness of the eyelid lining)
- Spots or rashes
- Vomiting
- Yellowish color or tint to the eyes or skin (jaundice)
- Difficulty in swallowing

Children with any of these symptoms should be isolated from the other children and should be observed for worsening conditions. The child should be within sight and hearing range of the adult in attendance and should be comforted until the parent arrives.

e. PARENT COMMUNICATION

Which brings us to another important weapon in the battle against illness — parent communication. During the pre–admission interview, explain to parents your procedures for maintaining good health in your center or home. Tell them —

(a) under which circumstances you will not accept a child into care,

(b) how and why you isolate a child who becomes ill,

(c) when they will be contacted to pick up a sick child, and

(d) if the child has a communicable disease, the point at which you will re-admit the child into care.

A chart outlining the various childhood illnesses, the symptoms, the contamination period, and the treatment required should be posted where the parents can see it. Your doctor and public health nurse will have copies of these charts that you can either copy or purchase to give to parents.

Most important, enlist the parents' help and support for your efforts. Ask them —

(a) to notify you if their child is exposed to a communicable disease,

(b) to have pre-arranged back-up care for those days when their child is ill,

(c) to keep you updated on their child's health and immunization record, the phone number for the parents and the emergency contact persons, doctor changes, anything that could affect the immediate and proper treatment of their ill child, and

(d) to help you in teaching their child about the importance of hand washing, personal grooming, and not sharing tissues.

Have each parent complete and return to you a copy of the child medical form shown in Sample #16.

If a parent requests that you administer medication to the child and you agree, you must secure the written consent of the parent or guardian. The written, signed, and dated instructions should provide you with information on the name of the medication, the exact times at which it is to be administered, the quantity to be given, and any special instructions, such as "on an empty stomach," "with a meal," and so on. You can use a medication permission form similar to the one shown in Sample #17.

Serve notice to parents that you mean business from the start by putting all your policies and procedures, from diapering to food preparation, from sanitizing to parent cooperation, in writing. Make certain every parent receives a copy of your health policy and that this policy is posted conspicuously.

f. THE HAZARD ZONE — YOUR HOME

Statistics prove that more children die each year from accidents than from any other cause. What makes these statistics so startling is that most of these accidents could have been prevented.

Prevention — applying measures that reduce the chances of an accident happening — is a key factor in keeping children safe. Following are some of the most common childhood accidents and some suggestions for reducing the potential for injury —

(a) falls,

(b) poisoning,

(c) drowning,

(d) choking,

(e) burns, and

(f) motor vehicle accidents.

1. Falls

When my son was about six months old, I put him in his automatic swinging chair so that I could prepare supper. Unfortunately, I did not take the time to properly fasten the seat strap and he fell, face first onto the kitchen linoleum, smashing his nose and forehead. Blood poured everywhere. There was no serious damage, I am happy to report, but there could have been. He could easily have landed on his head and broken his neck. My son was very fortunate. Many other children are not.

From the moment they are born, babies are susceptible to falls — off changing tables, out of strollers, down the stairs in walkers. As they grow, so does their capacity to find trouble. They climb over the crib rails and fall to the floor, fall off tricycles and swings, and trip going down stairs.

To help avoid falls —

(a) use barriers to keep small children off stairs,

(b) have a non-slippery surface on all floors,

(c) never leave a child unsecured for even a moment on anything above floor level, and

(d) tack down edges of carpets and throw rugs.

2. Poisoning

We would never think to take a swig of that pretty blue glass cleaner — but a child would. A child would also be tempted to eat the pill your mother-in-law dropped on the floor, or taste the pretty green foliage of your houseplant. One way a child learns about the world is to taste, drink, and eat things. Unfortunately, that natural curiosity could be deadly.

To help prevent poisonings —

(a) lock away all poisonous substances in your home,

(b) mark containers of poisonous goods with poison stickers, and

(c) contact your local poison control center for a list of all poisonous plants.

SAMPLE #16
CHILD MEDICAL FORM

_____

Child's full name_____
Last   First   Middle

Address:_____ Home phone #:_____

Date of birth:_____ Age:_____

Mother:_____ Work phone #:_____

Father: _____ Work phone #:_____

EMERGENCY CONTACT PERSON:

Name: _____ Phone #:_____

Name:_____ Phone #:_____

Child's doctor:_____ Phone #:_____

Child's health care #: _____

Hospital name:_____ Phone #:_____

ADDITIONAL INFORMATION (e.g., allergies, special medications, medical problems):
_____
_____

Medical:_____
_____

Physical:_____
_____

Developmental:_____
_____

Emotional:_____
_____
_____
_____

IMMUNIZATION RECORD:

(Contact your local Ministry of Health for complete details before filling in this area.)

Immunizations are up to date: YES_____NO_____

Has your child had: Does your child suffer from:
Measles   _____   Headaches   _____
German measles_____   Ear aches   _____
Chicken pox   _____   Stomach aches_____
Mumps   _____   Colds   _____
Whooping cough_____   Flu   _____
Other   _____   Sore throat   _____
                                   Other   _____

EMERGENCY MEDICAL CARE
I hereby grant permission for _____, to secure
the necessary emergency medical treatment needed by my
son/daugher_____,
in the event that I cannot be reached to otherwise authorize the same.

Date: _____   Parent signature:_____
                                     Parent signature:_____

SAMPLE #17
MEDICATION PERMISSION FORM

PERMISSION TO ADMINISTER MEDICATION FORM

Child's name: _____

Type of medication: _____

Name of medication: _____

Amount to be given: _____

Times to be given: _____

Precautions/Recommendations:_____
_____

Possible side effects: _____
_____

Physician's name:_____Phone #_____

Date to be discontinued:_____

Date:_____Parent's signature:_____
_____

3. Drowning

Did you know that a child can drown in a puddle only three inches deep? It's true. It doesn't take much water to form a hazard to a child, and there is water everywhere around us, dishwashing water in the sink, bathwater in the bathtub, drinking water in a pet's water dish, rainwater in the bottom of an old barrel.

To prevent drownings —

(a) never leave a child unattended around water,

(b) keep toilet lid down,

(c) be aware of the hazard water presents and try to reduce the danger by draining barrels and other places that water collects and by filling puddles, and

(d) make sure you know CPR in case of an accident.

4. Choking

The hot dog and grapes you are serving for lunch appear relatively harmless, and to an adult, they are. We know enough to chew our food thoroughly before we swallow it. A child, however, is not so experienced and often swallows foods whole. These large chunks of food can easily become lodged in the child's throat and cause choking. In addition, because a young child's initial reaction to anything is to put it in his or her mouth, a child can choke on lost buttons, toy car wheels, game pieces, money, and many other items.

To prevent choking —

(a) do not serve dangerous foods such as —

    (i) hot dogs,

    (ii) nuts,

    (iii) popcorn,

    (iv) grapes,

    (v) candy,

    (vi) fruit skins, and

    (vii) foods with nuts or bones,

(b) teach children to eat slowly and concentrate on chewing their food properly;

(c) cut larger foods into child-size bites; and

(d) learn the Heimlich maneuver, particularly as it is performed on children.

5. Burns

The pot handle sticking out from the edge of the stove looks, from a child's point of view, like a perfect place to grab for support. One tug, and there's boiling soup over little Tara's head and shoulders. The hot iron, left for one minute while Dad answers the phone, can too easily come crashing down on a toddler grasping for support from the shaky ironing board. Scalding water from the tap is yet another hazard.

To avoid burns —

(a) turn hot-water temperature down to below 120°F (48.9°C),

(b) keep hot objects up and out of the reach of children, including their cords,

(c) keep pot handles turned in over the stove,

(d) never serve food that is scalding hot,

(e) install barriers around all heaters and radiators, and

(f) never leave children unattended in a room with a hot object.

6. Motor vehicle accidents

Car accidents are so frequent in our lives now that we almost take them for granted. Most people will be in a car accident at some point in their lives. But even a minor accident can have tragic consequences if someone in the car is not wearing a seat belt or child restraint. It is now common knowledge that seat belts and child car seats save lives, yet you still see people driving without seat belts and allowing their children to ride unsecured. "Oh, I'm just going down to the corner store," "Little Johnnie fusses when I belt him in," or "It's too much trouble to fiddle around with all those straps and buckles" are some of the excuses you hear.

To prevent injuries in case of an accident —

(a) have a child restraint appropriate to the age of the child for every child that will ride in the car,

(b) make sure these are installed correctly,

(c) make sure that they are used correctly,

(d) insist that children remain buckled in even when the vehicle is not moving, and

(e) teach children about the importance of seat-belt use, particularly through good example.

7. Other dangers

Sharp corners on furniture, doilies hanging where an infant can grab at them, cords waiting to be tugged on, sliding doors that are not secured, an ashtray left to a child's curiosity — all are accidents waiting to happen. It is up to you, as a provider of child care, to keep a constant watch for potential dangers and do your best to remove them. One of the best ways to child-proof an area is to get down on your hands and knees to "child's-eye level" and crawl around, thinking like a child looking for something interesting to grab, mouth, or poke a finger into.

Here are some general tips on safety:

- Never leave a child unattended.

- Never lock children in a room.

- Take first aid and CPR courses.

- Define your first aid policies.

- Post a first aid chart where it is easily accessible.

- Always use equipment according to manufacturer's instructions

- Take the time to tie that shoelace, buckle that buckle, or tighten that bolt.

- Never tie pacifiers or other objects around a child's neck.

Worksheet #14 is a safety checklist for you to use when child-proofing your home. If the checklist seems trite and exhaustive, remember that meticulousness could spare a child's life.

g. OUTDOOR SAFETY

Outdoor accidents leading to injury happen as frequently as indoor accidents, so you need to be aware of the problems that can occur while children play and how to prevent serious injuries from occurring.

The first thing you should do when taking children outside to play is make a safety check of the play area, be it your day care's outdoor play area or the local park. Look for signs of broken glass, bottles, and cans. Check for broken or dangerous equipment such as threadbare swings, loose screws, shaky anchors, or sharp edges. Protruding nuts, bolts, or nails are also dangerous as the children can cut themselves or catch their clothing and become caught in the equipment. Check sand boxes for animal feces and place the area off limits if any are found. If your day care has a sandbox, make sure it has a snug-fitting lid.

If you are in your own yard, ensure that all gate latches are working properly, the fence is free of splinters and cracks, the equipment is checked weekly for loose or broken parts, and junk, like old car parts, are kept outside the fence where the children cannot reach them.

When you visit a new play area, take along your tape measure to measure the depth of the surface under the equipment. Equipment areas should have a cushion-type surface (sand, wood chips, tire pieces) at least 8" to 12" (20 cm to 30 cm) deep. Equipment built on cement, asphalt, grass,

WORKSHEET #14
SAFETY CHECKLIST

[ ] Posted by every telephone the number for:

_____ Police department

_____ Fire department

_____ Ambulance

_____ Hospital

_____ Poison control center

_____ Physician

[ ] In working order:

_____ Smoke detectors

_____ Flashlights

_____ Fire extinquisher

[ ] Practiced monthly, emergency evacuation plan for:

_____ Fire

_____ Earthquake

_____ Fire extinquisher

_____ Severe weather

_____ Serious accident

[ ] Locked-up:

_____ Medicines

_____ Poisonous substances

_____ Matches, lighters

_____ Freezers

_____ Window screens

_____ Patio doors

_____ Cleaning supplies

_____ Scissors, knives

_____ Guns and ammunition

_____ Gates

_____ Screen doors

[ ] Up and out of harm's way:

_____ Perfumes, after–shaves, hygiene products

_____ Nail polish and remover

_____ Poisonous plants

_____ Cords from window blinds

_____ Portable heaters

_____ Make-up

_____ Crib mobiles

[ ] Covered securely:

_____ Electrical outlets

_____ Diaper pails

_____ Wood stoves

_____ Garbage containers

_____ Sharp corners on furniture

_____ Water tables

_____ Barbeque pits

[ ] Stairways have handrails for both adults and children and are uncluttered.

[ ] Hot water is below 120°F (49°C).

[ ] Checked weekly:

_____ Toys for loose and broken parts

_____ Safety gates

_____ Crib slides, latches and hardware

_____ Playpens

_____ Strollers

_____ Car seats

_____ High chairs

[ ] Checked monthly:

_____ All equipment

_____ Climbers

_____ Paint, for chips

_____ Tricycles

[ ] Checked daily:

_____ Floors for small objects

_____ pins, needles, glass

_____ plastic bags

or rocks is not suitable for outdoor play, it is simply too dangerous.

Your tape measure will also come in handy for measuring the space between the bars on any equipment that has bars. These spaces should be less than 3½" (9 cm) or wider than 9" (24 cm) to prevent a child's head from being trapped in the bars.

On hot summer days, test the slide bed before allowing children to go down. The steel type slide in particular, is extremely dangerous as it stores the sun's heat and can actually burn a child. If there is a swimming or wading pool at the park or in your play area, never let the children go near the pool unattended. Be sure to take along hats and sunscreen, and look for shady areas where the children can get out of the sun.

It is always a good idea to take along a first aid kit when venturing away from your home.

Finally, teach the children a few positive playground rules:

(a) Only one child goes down the slide at a time.

(b) The merry-go-round has to stop completely before you can stand up.

(c) We sit on the swings so we do not fall off.

(d) We all hold hands when we are crossing the street.

h. FIRE SAFETY

Fact: In most fires, people have only three minutes to get to safety.

In other words, you have to be able to get all the children out of your home within three minutes after your smoke detector or alarm goes off. That is a tall order if everyone starts crying and screaming. That is why you must practice your fire-drill procedures at least once a month. You and the children have to know beyond a shadow of a doubt how to get out of your building safely and quickly. Getting them out alive is your responsibility. Here's how:

(a) Make sure exit passageways are clear at all times.

(b) Post your evacuation plans in each room, but know them by heart.

(c) When you conduct fire drills, make note of problem areas, then work to correct them.

(d) Aim for a 90-second evacuation. More than that and you are jeopardizing the lives of everyone.

(e) Enlist the help of your fire department when setting up your fire-evacuation plans. Inquire about fire-evacuation classes to learn about getting infants out using cribs or blanket drags; how and where to look for a lost or frightened child who did not come out of the building. Practice these techniques on a yearly basis so you don't forget them.

(f) Learn how to use fire extinguishers and how to call in an alarm.

(g) Pick a location outside the building and away from the danger where you can regroup with the children and do a head count to be sure everyone got out.

(h) To help the children understand the need for monthly fire drills, borrow books from your library that explain these routines, books like *The Little Fire Engine* by Lois Lenski and *The Little Fireman* by Margaret Wise Brown.

(i) If your fire alarm or smoke detector goes off, don't assume it is a malfunction, even if you don't see fire or smell smoke. It is surprising how many people dismiss an alarm as a false one and blandly go about their business. Get yourself and the children to safety first, poke around for the cause of the alarm later.

(j) Respect your yearly fire inspection. Learn from it. Talk to the fire marshal and implement his or her recommendations.

Musical Chairs

This game requires at least four players.

Object of the game: to be the last one sitting on a chair when the music stops.

How to play: Chairs are lined up either in a row or back to back. Start out with one less chair than the number of children playing. The children move slowly around the chairs while an adult plays some music. As soon as the music stops, each child must find a chair to sit on. The child without a chair steps out of the game. The adult removes one chair and starts the music. This goes on until only one child and one chair are left. When the music stops, the first one to sit in the remaining chair wins the game.

13

NUTRITION

Recently, both Canada and the United States have released new and updated versions of their food guides. These new-generation guides place a greater emphasis on eating grains such as rice, pasta, breads, and cereals, and fiber foods such as fruits and vegetables. Permitted on today's menus are such things as peanut butter and the occasional fast-food burger.

Although these changes reflect a change in today's lifestyles, one thing remains the same: healthy meals should contain at least one food from each of the four food groups. And, according to most licensing regulations, the meals you serve must contain a third of the daily allowance for each group.

a. THE FOOD GUIDE

In all likelihood you have, sometime during your schooling, studied the food guide and the four food groups: grains and cereals, fruits and vegetables, dairy products, and meat and meat alternatives. The purpose of the food guide is to make it easier for people to follow a diet that is high in the nutrients the body needs most to stay healthy, without having to completely understand the complexities and nutrient values of every food item. The guide lists recommended daily servings of each group for children and adults. This is known as a foundation diet. It is like the baseline in child care. It represents the minimum standard by which a body can sustain itself. But just as you are not going to be contented to provide the minimum standard of child care, you should strive to do better than the minimum standard of diet. By choosing the foods that rate highest on the list of recommended foods in each group, you can provide optimum nutrition for the children in your care.

Table #3 lists examples of the foods that belong to each food group.

This is by no means a complete list, but it does exemplify the options you have when you are making up your menus. Many of these foods can be served in combination, such as spaghetti and meatballs.

b. MENU PLANNING

Back during my university days, I worked part time in the dietary department of a local hospital. This experience taught me a great deal about menu planning and some of what I learned can be applied to your own menu planning.

When a patient entered the hospital, he or she received a visit from the dietitian who talked about the hospital's menus and inquired about the individual's dietary needs. Often, if the patient had a particular way of eating, like a preference for only certain foods or a diet based on his or her cultural background, this was noted on the menu and the hospital would do its best to accommodate the patient.

You might want to approach your menu planning in much the same fashion. Talk to the parents during the pre–admission interview about your menu and about their child's particular eating habits or special diet. Note his or her likes and dislikes and

**TABLE #3
THE FOUR FOOD GROUPS**

RECOMMENDED DAILY SERVINGS FOR CHILDREN:			
FRUITS AND VEGETABLES	BREADS AND CEREALS	MEAT AND POULTRY ALTERNATIVES	DAIRY PRODUCTS
cantaloupe	whole-wheat bread	poultry	2% milk
oranges	crackers	fish	cheese
grapefruit	bread sticks	eggs	yogurt
strawberries	oatmeal	lean pork	puddings
bananas	muffins	lean beef	cottage cheese
carrots	pasta	peanut butter	milk shake
broccoli	waffles	lentils	ice cream
tomatoes	rice	legumes	macaroni and cheese
turnips		tofu	
4 - 6	3 - 6	3 - 4	3 - 4

try on occasion to serve these favored foods. Menus, both daily and weekly, should be posted for parents.

Before you set out to do any meal planning, you might want to consult with a nutritionist who can give you a basic outline to follow, as well as some tips on how to help the children develop good eating habits. Your local licensing board should have the names and telephone numbers of nutrition consultants in your area.

It is not necessary for you to sit down every Friday and try to figure out what to feed the children for the coming week. Instead, use a rotating menu plan like a hospital does. Work out four or five weekly menus and then rotate them. This allows you to vary the foods the children eat without going to a lot of work. It is relatively easy to change a menu on occasion by substituting certain foods on a given day, such as seasonal fresh fruit instead of canned fruit or fresh carrots instead of frozen, or to incorporate special items like birthday cakes without having to re-schedule your entire weekly plan.

When creating a menu, pay close attention to the recommended daily requirements for the four food groups. Each meal must contain one-third to one-half of a child's daily nutritional requirements in all four food groups. See the Weekly Menu in Sample #18 for an idea of how daily food guide requirements can be met. At the same time, try to make foods interesting, appealing, colorful, and fun to eat. Scattered throughout this book at the chapter openings are a variety of recipes for dishes that keep kids in mind.

Day cares in the United States may be eligible to receive funds through the Child Care Food Program to help with obtaining, preparing, and serving meals that meet the U.S. Department of Agriculture requirements. For more information on where to apply in your state, contact:

Food and Nutrition Service
U.S. Department of Agriculture
Washington, DC 20250

c. MEALTIMES

Mealtimes should be enjoyable times for children. They should be times to relax and to quietly socialize with friends, peers, and adults. When you schedule the meals you will provide, give consideration to the age groups you have and how you can work these groups into a satisfactory lunch and breakfast timetable. For example, you could feed the babies at 11:30 a.m., the toddlers at 12:00 noon, and the preschoolers around 12:30. When you have these schedules figured out, note their times in your daily and weekly schedules and in your policy statement. Mealtimes should include breakfast, a midmorning snack, lunch, an afternoon snack, and if you offer it, supper as well.

This is the time to lay a foundation for good table manners, so create some simple rules for children to follow when eating meals. For example, tell the children that eating is only done sitting down, not standing, playing, or jumping up and down. Insist that they sit at the table and encourage them to concentrate on the food they are eating.

d. GETTING CHILDREN TO EAT

Children may not always eat what we put in front of them. Their appetites change like the weather, the foods they are served at home do not even closely resemble what you prepare, and some children are just plain fussy eaters. Nonetheless, it is up to you to help the children understand the value of good nutrition and healthful eating habits — that what goes into their bodies today could very well effect how they'll feel tomorrow and that the sticky junk food may have to be drilled off at the dentist office. Maybe the younger ones won't understand all that, but they will gather some idea of what you are talking about when you tell them that it's the milk that helps their bones grow big and strong and the carrots that help them to see the stars at night.

Remember, too, that children learn by example. They watch us grown-ups very

SAMPLE #18
WEEKLY MENU

Meal component	Monday	Tuesday	Wednesday	Thursday	Friday
Breakfast: Fruit or juice Bread or alternative Milk	Apple sauce French toast Milk	Fruit cup Oatmeal with apples and cinnamon Milk	Pineapple juice Dry cereal Milk	Banana slices Toast with peanut butter Milk	Orange juice Raisin muffin Scrambled egg Milk
Snack: A.M. Fresh fruit or vegetables Bread or alternative Meat Milk	Peanut butter and honey balls Orange juice	Cheese Ritz crackers Apple juice	Muffin Applesauce Milk	Sliced vegetables Crackers Milk	Luncheon meat Toast Milk
P.M.	Graham crackers W a t e r m e l o n chunks Milk	Vanilla wafers Peanut butter Milk	Banana pops Milk	Cheese chunks Apple chunks Milk	Fruit tray Vanilla wafers Milk
Lunch: Meat or meat alternative Bread or alternative Fruit or vegetable Milk	Fish sticks Tater chunks Sliced veggies Toast Milk	Chicken Noodle Soup Cheese sandwich Orange sections Milk	Beef patty Rice Beans in tomato sauce Fruit salad Milk	Hot dog on a bun Beans in tomato sauce Fruit salad Milk	Chicken sand-wich Carrot and celery sticks Apple chunks Muffin Milk

carefully and try to be like us whenever they can. So it is important for you to demonstrate good eating habits in front of the children. Eat slowly. Enjoy your food. Participate in the social gathering before you. And always eat a little of everything on your plate.

Try to include the older children in your food preparation. This is a great time to talk to them about the food guide and its components and why each of the four food groups is so important. Letting them have a hand in preparing the food they will eat may encourage them to eat it. They can —

(a) set the table,

(b) wash the fruits and vegetables,

(c) hold the hand beater,

(d) cut soft foods, and

(e) spread soft butter.

Often it takes a creative touch to get children to eat. Here are some helpful hints that might encourage better eating habits:

(a) Serve meals at regularly scheduled times.

(b) Make mealtime a happy, relaxing time.

(c) Sit and eat with the children. Your good habits can't help but rub off.

(d) Do not use food as a punishment or a reward.

(e) Do not force children to eat. They know when they are hungry and when they have had enough.

(f) Find out what some of their favorite foods are and then consider adjusting your menu to include these foods.

(g) Serve finger foods such as carrot sticks, cheese fingers, and sliced fruit.

(h) Introduce new foods regularly but singularly. Do not force a child to try a food until he is ready.

(i) Keep serving sizes relative to the child's age.

e. INFANT FEEDINGS

Most centers request that parents supply all infant formula and juice feedings. It is simply too time-consuming to be sterilizing bottles and formula. When an infant enters your child-care program, you must receive a written feeding schedule from the parents. Utilizing a daily information form on which you mark down when and how much a baby eats during the day is a good way to keep track of these feedings. A copy of this form should be given to the parents when they come to pick up their child.

Keep in mind that the feeding period should be a relaxing time when the infant is held in your arms. This is important because a baby needs not only food, but love and affection from his or her primary caregiver — you.

As the baby matures, solid foods will be introduced into his or her diet. Discuss this process with the parents and work out a schedule of foods and feedings that will make the transition from bottle feeding easier for all concerned. Be sure to properly refrigerate infant formulas and never serve foods directly from the jars. Open jars of infant food must be dated and consumed within 48 hours. Outdated food should be discarded.

f. SPECIAL DIETS

Unless you have agreed otherwise, parents are usually responsible for providing meals and snacks for the child who requires a special diet. Instructions should be included with these meals. You must be aware of what reactions a child may have if the wrong food is ingested and what to do if a reaction occurs. You will be responsible for properly storing the food supplied by the parent and should complete a daily record of the child's food intake. This record should be given to the parent when the child is picked up.

Happy Face Snack

Rice cakes

Processed cheese spread

Cucumber, olive slices, or raisins for eyes

Red peppers, tomato sections, shelled sunflower seeds for mouth and nose

- Cut the tomato or red pepper into bite-size pieces. (If you use a tomato, remove seeds and inner pulp.)
- Slice olives or cucumbers. Spread processed cheese spread over rice cake.
- Let the children make their own faces.

14
CHILDREN WITH SPECIAL NEEDS

What do you think of when you hear the words "Special Olympics"? Chances are the first thing that pops into your mind is "disabled." But if you think a little harder, you'll begin to visualize people with real courage and determination. Happy, bright, smiling faces come into focus. And then, in the background, you see dedicated teenagers, famous personalities, ordinary people, and loving parents and siblings coaching, encouraging, and befriending these special members of our community who have, until recently, been all but forgotten — people who were seldom seen in public, let alone the focus of so much attention. The Special Olympics have helped to change our perception of what it means to be disabled.

The same approach is being applied to day care. Children with special needs are being integrated into programs across the continent and the results are proving favorable for both the disabled child and the other children. Our goal should be to help children develop into independent and capable beings regardless of their "abilities" or "disabilities." Welcoming special-needs children into your day care gives them a sense of motivation, of wanting to do more of the same activities their peers do, of finding themselves despite their limitations. Most children, when exposed to special-needs children at an early age, develop a sense of appreciation and empathy for those who are different in some ways that will help them grow into caring people.

a. MAKING THE DECISION TO CARE FOR SPECIAL CHILDREN

If a parent approaches you with a request for you to provide care for a disabled child, don't dismiss the possibility before you have had a chance to meet with the child and his or her family, to discuss the child's disability, and to inquire with your local health services office about the child's specific type of disability and the possibility of integrating the child into your program. Seek the advice of the child's pediatrician or specialist.

If, after these consultations, you feel confidence in your ability to provide care for the child, you can take him or her in on the same trial basis as with any other child. This will give you a chance to see whether you can meet this challenge.

There is no real reason a child with some degree of disability cannot attend your day care. You may need to do a bit more planning as a child with a handicap may need more assistance in reaching the development goals you have established for the children in your day care. Know what you can expect in terms of the child's overall development and, through your program, help the child to reach or exceed these expectations.

Periodically, you should review the child's progress. Keep accurate records of the child's progress. Have an agency that deals with the child's type of disability come in to assess the care you are providing as well as the child's progress under that care. Discuss their concerns and implement their suggestions as best you can. Provide this special child with every opportunity to succeed.

b. HANDLING THE ISSUE WITH THE PARENTS OF YOUR OTHER CHILDREN

Many parents, because of a lack of knowledge about disabled children, may be uncomfortable with your decision to bring a special-needs child into your care. You should reassure them that this decision will not in any way effect the quality of care their child will receive. Hold a parent meeting to discuss the disability and to explain that you have done everything possible to ensure a smooth integration. Explain the pluses for both the disabled child and their child. Have a qualified specialist discuss the situation with them. Be open and frank and do your best to address all their concerns and answer all their questions. In time, they will see that a special-needs child is no threat to their child and that he or she may turn out to be one of their child's best buddies.

c. READYING YOUR HOME

To care properly for the special-needs child, you may need to make some adjustments in your day care facilities. For example, if the child uses a wheelchair, your home will need to be wheelchair accessible. This includes wheelchair access in and out of the house, adaptations to the bathroom, and possibly other changes. Consult your licensing regulations for these requirements and contact local associations for the disabled to find out more about making your home accessible.

If the child will require a good deal of individual attention, you may need to hire someone to help. To help cover the cost of hiring an assistant for this purpose, funding such as special state, provincial, or federal grants may be available. Contact agencies that specialize in the special needs of your particular disabled child about assistance with your staffing requirements or the cost of any additional equipment that may be necessary to properly care for the child.

Simon Says

Can be played with any size group.

Object of the game: to do only those things that Simon "says" to do.

How to play: The children gather round "Simon," (usually an adult), and must do as Simon says. If they do what the leader says without "Simon" telling them to and they are caught, they must leave the game.

For example, the leader says "Simon says...touch your nose." All the children must touch their noses. This carries on with all sorts of actions from jumping up and down to standing on one leg, until the leader says "Do this..." Any children who "do this" without "Simon" saying so, have to sit out until the game starts over. The last child left in the game is the winner and he or she is the new "Simon Says."

15

PARENTS: PARTNERS IN CHILD CARE

A partnership is comprised of two or more persons working together towards a common goal; in this case, the provision of quality child care. Your partnership with parents means that you are not going it alone, that you have someone to discuss things with and share the responsibilities. But it also means that they have a say, a big say, in how their child is cared for by you. If you and the parents of the children in your care are to establish a good partnership, you must each understand what the other is doing and why. To achieve this, you need good communication in both directions.

a. STARTING OUT ON THE RIGHT FOOT

Your first contact with parents is during the pre–admission interview. At this point, you should establish a sort of camaraderie, a mutual respect for each other's expectations, hopes, and wants for the child. You discuss your program, your ways of dealing with discipline, your illness policy, and all the other particulars a parent needs to know in order to make an informed decision as to whether the child will be happy in your care and whether they can live with your house rules. In turn, encourage the parent to talk at length about their child, his or her likes and dislikes, diet, special requirements, disposition. It is a good idea to make notes about the child during this interview. Explain to the parent that this helps you to take better care of the child.

Let parents know that you try to do the very best you can in keeping them informed about their child's progress and that it may sometimes be necessary for you to discuss with them problems or concerns you may have. Explain that when this happens, you are not complaining about their parenting skills or judging them in any way, but are turning to them for advice and support and that their insights and suggestions may help in solving the problem. Advise parents that addressing concerns when they are small will save a lot of heartache and disgruntled feelings should the problem suddenly get out of hand.

Let parents know their cooperation is imperative for quality care. Ask them to let you know when they drop off their child if their child is feeling ill or upset and if there are problems in the family that could help you to understand why the child is feeling that way. Offer to help if you think it is appropriate and let them know they can phone you any time there is a problem.

When the formalities are out of the way, you can relax and get to know each other better. Show the parent around your home, making them feel comfortable and welcome. Take them through your reception area, making a special effort to point out your parent information board, your daily communication or attendance forms, your envelopes for relaying messages, and your calendar with appointments to discuss problems and for regularly scheduled caregiver/parent conferences.

b. KEEP THEM INVOLVED

Once you have established a good basis for your partnership, the parents may tend to relax and just leave you to do your job. While such confidence may be flattering, don't let them become distanced from their child's care. They need to be involved with what is going on. To involve parents, try some of the following ideas:

- Make up a monthly newsletter. Involve the children in this activity (language development). Ask them what they want to tell Mom and Dad about what they've been doing and what they have planned for next month. They can mention funny things that happened. Include a few of the children's drawings and a Reminder Column to keep parents up to date on activities and problems that need rectifying.

- Ask parents to bring in odds and ends from home. Boxes, bread tags, leftover yarn and fabric scraps, pieces of lumber, even toys the older children have outgrown would be most welcome.

- Plan a monthly picnic or potluck dinner where everyone brings some food and gets together for a visit.

- Keep a suggestion box in the reception area. Check it weekly and make changes as you see fit. Bring the suggestions up at parent meetings. Compromise on some issues if necessary.

- Post a "Visits Welcome Anytime" sign to encourage parents to drop by on their lunch hour or stay for a coffee when they come to pick up their child.

For more ideas on ways to get parents involved in your program, you might want to subscribe to *What's Working in Parent Involvement*, a newsletter published by The Parent Institute, P.O. Box 7474, Fairfax Station, VA 22039-7474. Another good newsletter to subscribe to is *Parent Care, Your Child Care Newsline*. This publication keeps parents up to date on the latest child-care news and helps them understand the many issues that affect child care. Contact, CanDan Publishing Co., P.O. Box 126, Canal Flats, British Columbia V0B 1B0.

c. PROBLEM SOLVING

Resolving problems with parents is an area you should approach positively. Take the emphasis away from the problem and focus on the solution instead. For example, if a parent is neglecting his or her responsibility to keep you supplied with diapers, you could say "Gee, I am having a bit of trouble maintaining my diaper stock. Do you suppose you could check your child's supply for me and bring some in if she needs them?" This takes the blame off the parent and addresses the problem instead. Or, if a parent neglects to take the time to fill out the daily information sheet, you could say offhandedly, "You know, I find it difficult sometimes to care for the children when I don't know how they slept the night before or if they are teething. I really need to explain to the parents again just why these forms are so important" and then leave it at that. Chances are the parent will get the hint.

Here are some tips on solving problems:

(a) Be consistent. Your house rules must apply to every family. If you send one child home with a cough you must send home every child with the same problem. If parents see discrepancies in the way you run your program, you are certain to have problems.

(b) Look for the right opportunity to approach parents. A parent who is having a bad day or who is running late is not a parent to corner with a problem. The same goes for you. If you are angry or upset you are in no frame of mind to positively discuss any problem.

153

(c) Make sure you have your facts straight before you approach a parent. If you haven't been paid for the last pay period, have your books out to prove that fact.

(d) Give the parents their day in court. There may be a simple explanation as to why the parent forgot the diapers and why Johnny is deliberately breaking all the toys.

(e) Work out a suitable solution to the problem. For example, Johnny's toy-breaking may be the result of a new baby in the family. With the parent's help, he may in time settle down and life will get back to normal. In the meantime, the parent agrees to replace all the toys Johnny destroys.

(f) When a problem is in the process of being resolved, give the parents a progress report. Keeping each other informed makes it seem that you are fighting a common enemy — the problem — rather than each other.

Mr. Mouse's Fruit Salad

Lettuce leaves

Cottage cheese

Carrots

Tinned pear halves

Raisins, pitted prunes

- Cut carrots into thin slices for whiskers and tail.
- Place lettuce leaves on plate, add cottage cheese on top.
- Put pear on the cottage cheese, flat side down. Insert carrot whiskers and tail.
- Use raisins for nose and eyes, pitted prunes for ears.

16
KEEPING RECORDS

I know what you are thinking — keeping records of any kind is a tedious prospect and you'd rather just skip it. The truth is, you cannot operate a business without records. As a day-care operator, you will need the standard financial records as well as specific information filed on the children you care for and your facility.

a. FINANCIAL RECORDS

Your financial records will include income and expense logs and other essential money matters. These will constitute a set of records that will allow you to see, at a glance, where you stand in terms of profit, where you need to take belt-tightening measures, and where you are holding your own.

Before you begin any formal bookkeeping system, you would be wise to seek the help of an accountant who can assist you in setting up your books and doing your taxes. Since tax laws are complex and differ in each region, it would be fruitless for me to go into detail about specific aspects of your income tax. There are many books on tax and small businesses that can help with some of your questions and concerns. The more you learn from the most current titles, the easier it will be for you to understand your tax obligations.

To keep track of your finances, you will need to set up some kind of ledger system. This can be done in the old-fashioned way, in actual ledgers, or in the high-tech way, on computer. As a day-care operator, you will be able to claim a variety of business expenses, which should lessen your total taxes

payable. Therefore, it is in your best interests to keep accurate records of all your expenses and revenues.

Generally, the financial records for an average day care are much simpler than for many other types of businesses. You will be receiving income from only one or two sources, and your expenses will be confined to providing one type of service.

1. What is a business expense?

For an expense to be a legitimate business expense, it must meet the following criteria:

(a) It must have been an expense incurred in the process of earning business income or in the hope of earning business income.

(b) It must be reasonable.

For example, if you bought a sign for your day care that would go on your front lawn, that would be a legitimate business expense, as long as the cost is reasonable. A sign that cost $10,000 would not be a reasonable business expense for a small day care.

Business expenses can be classified into three categories:

(a) Direct

(b) Capital

(c) Prorated

Any money spent strictly on your business is a direct business expense. For example, if you purchased crayons for the children to use, that would be a direct expense. Other direct expenses might include —

- food,

- supplies,

- toys,

- office supplies,

- special day-care insurance,

- bank charges,

- professional fees, and

- advertising.

Larger items are usually classified as capital expenses. Generally, these are items from which your day care will derive a benefit over a long period of time. Capital expenses are charged to the business over a number of years rather than being charged entirely in the year of purchase. An example might be an adventure playground for your back yard. Other capital expenses might include —

- furniture used only for your day care (crib, desk, dining table), and

- equipment or expensive toys.

A prorated expense is one that can be proportionally assigned to your business. Some prorated expenses might include —

- utilities,

- rent,

- property taxes,

- telephone,

- auto expenses, and

- renovations or house repairs.

Always check with your accountant about classifications for direct, capital, and prorated expenses, as what qualifies as a direct or capital expense, what can be prorated, by how much, and under what conditions are all complicated matters.

2. Expense records

You should always keep every receipt you receive for money you pay out for your business and keep your personal and business purchases separate. If you are shopping for groceries, for example, it is better to have the cashier ring through your personal groceries separate from the groceries you are buying for the day care. Then you can file the receipt from your day-care groceries.

Make a note on each receipt of exactly what was purchased. Many stores are not equipped with sophisticated computers that print out each item you purchase, so it is up to you to do the notating. Your notes will help you decide which expense category to file the receipt under.

If you do not get a receipt from the vendor (for example, at a garage sale), make a memo with the date, purchase price, description of the item, purpose of purchase, and who you bought it from. Then ask the vendor to sign the memo.

All the receipts for each month can be stored in one envelope marked with the month and year. At the beginning of a new month, you start a new envelope and file the old one. While you do not have to send these receipts in with your tax forms, you must have them as proof should the tax department ever question your claim. Failure to produce these or any forms pertinent to your tax return could result in serious consequences.

To record your expenses, set up a ledger with columns for each type of expense you will be recording. You should be able to use the same categories you set up for your estimated operating budget in chapter 5. Enter each expense by date, vendor, and item. All items are entered under "Total" *and* again under the appropriate category (see Sample #19).

At the end of the month, you add up the "Total" column to get your total expenses for the month. Add up the totals in the other

SAMPLE #19
MONTHLY EXPENSE RECORD

Magicland Day Care Monthly Expenses — May, 199-

#	DATE	Expense	Supp	Food	Util	Tel	Mort	Acco	Law	Ad	Misc	Total
01	05-01	First Bank	Mortgage				145.00					145.00
02	05-03	BuyNow	Groceries	34.50								34.50
03	05-04	Acme Hydro	Power		22.60							22.60
04	05-07	Bains Inc	Accounting					50.00				50.00
05	05-07	State Tel	Telephone			6.25						6.25
06	05-10	BuyNow	Groc. & supp.	24.62							22.25	46.87
07	05-13	The News	Classified ad							15.00		15.00
08	05-17	BuyNow	Groceries	35.73								35.73
09	05-18	Shell	Gas		12.00							12.00
10	05-21	Play Time	Play dough								4.69	4.69
11	05-24	Cal Cable	Cablevision		6.00							6.00

columns to find out how much you spent on each category for the month. If you add up all the totals of the category columns, this amount should equal the amount of your total expenses. If not, you have made an error entering or adding something. This is a good check for your system.

At the end of the year, prepare an expense summary sheet similar to the one shown in Sample #20. Enter the month, the total expenses for that month, and the total expense in each category for that month. Then add up the columns to get a total expense amount for the year and total expenses in each category for the year.

Remember that your accountant will be charging you by the hour to check over your books, so the neater and more complete your records are, the less time the accountant will need to spend on your books and the less money it will cost you.

3. Revenue records

To keep track of your business revenue or income, you should set up a monthly income journal noting the date, the source of income, the item covered, and the amount. Most likely, your sole or major source of income will be parent-paid fees, but you may also receive money from government subsidies or food programs, so these also need to be recorded (see Sample #21). A miscellaneous column can be used to record any income that is irregular; for example, in Sample #21, it appears that the Sidhus forgot to renew their supply of diapers and the day-care operator had to purchase some. The $15.34 income represents their reimbursement of this expense.

At the end of the year, prepare a revenue summary as you did for your expenses. The total revenue for each month should be entered and the total revenue for the year calculated.

Always maintain an accurate daily attendance record for each child. This will help you to keep track of what each parent owes you. Make sure parents receive receipts for all moneys paid to you.

For more information on keeping your business finance records, see *Basic Accounting for the Small Business*, another title in the Self-Counsel Series.

4. Your business account

Make sure you open a special business account for your day care. A standard checking account should be sufficient. All business income should be kept in this account and all business purchases made from this account. This account should be used for business transactions only.

Make all payments and purchases by check, and record them in the checkbook accordingly by date, amount, payee, and what the payment was for. Mark the check number and the date paid on bills and invoices.

b. CHILD RECORDS

If you look at your licensing requirements, you may find that your licensing board has taken the liberty of mandating your records system. This, at least, gives you the minimum information you must keep on file. Obviously, you will let those requirements be your guide in setting up your system.

Whatever your licensing requirements, you will need to open a file for each child who enters your care. That file should contain the following:

(a) Child information sheet (see Sample #22)

(b) Child–care agreement (see Sample #13)

(c) Child medical form (see Sample #16)

(d) Medication permission form, if necessary (see Sample #17)

Magicland Day Care Expense Summary

#	Month	Total	Food	Suppl	Util	Tel	Mort	Law	Acco	Ad	Misc.
1	Jan	453.88	110.30	24.65	42.50	8.00	245.00	00.00	00.00	00.00	23.43
2	Feb	450.67	102.34	31.00	40.21	8.00	245.00	00.00	00.00	10.67	13.45
3	Mar	512.55	118.10	34.76	39.20	8.00	245.00	50.00	00.00	00.00	17.49
4	Apr	479.03	123.98	22.23	37.97	8.00	245.00	00.00	30.00	00.00	11.85
5	May	440.82	101.24	24.00	39.63	8.00	245.00	00.00	00.00	00.00	22.95
6	Jun	483.93	124.43	38.00	36.50	8.00	245.00	00.00	00.00	00.00	32.00
7	Jul	450.06	98.48	25.21	32.96	8.00	245.00	00.00	00.00	13.00	27.41
8	Aug	419.03	99.23	19.04	31.84	8.00	245.00	00.00	00.00	00.00	15.92
9	Sept	424.80	95.00	26.94	32.84	8.00	245.00	00.00	00.00	00.00	17.02
10	Oct	451.16	97.99	31.39	34.72	8.00	245.00	25.00	00.00	00.00	9.06
11	Nov	449.16	102.23	35.72	35.22	8.00	245.00	00.00	00.00	00.00	22.99
12	Dec	428.16	105.44	19.34	39.88	8.00	245.00	00.00	00.00	00.00	10.50
		5443.25	1278.70	6332.28	443.47	96.00	2940.00	75.00	30.00	23.67	224.07

#	DATE	SOURCE	TOTAL	FEES	SUBSIDY	FOOD PRO.	MISC.
			Magicland Day Care Monthly Revenue Record — May, 199-				
1	05-01	Smith - May	800.00	800.00			
2	05-01	Sidhu - May	850.00	850.00			
3	05-01	Jones - May	650.00	650.00			
4	05-01	Keller - May	400.00	400.00			
5	05-01	Chan - May	800.00	800.00			
6	05-04	Govern. (Keller) - May	400.00		400.00		
7	05-14	Food pro. - May	50.00			50.00	
8	05-20	Jones - jacket	25.00				25.00
9	05-27	Sidhu - diapers	15.34				15.34
			3990.34				

(e) Medication administered form, if necessary (see Sample #23)

(f) Accident, injury, and illness reports, if any (see Sample #24)

(g) Transportation permission form (see Sample #8)

(h) Daily information forms (see Sample #25)

These files must be kept strictly confidential. No one except you and your licensing authority should have access to these files.

c. FACILITY RECORDS

Your facility records should include the following:

(a) Licensing records

(b) Fire inspection logs

(c) Building inspection logs

(d) Sanitation inspection logs

(e) Zoning compliances

(f) Insurance records

(g) Copies of your emergency procedures for fire and other disasters

(h) Names and phone numbers of —

    (i) the public health nurse,

    (ii) a nutrition consultant,

    (iii) a child development specialist, and

    (iv) medical personnel who assist the center.

This may not cover all the forms and information you may be required to keep on file. Discuss your record-keeping system with your local licensing office to get a better understanding of the requirements in your area.

d. EMPLOYEE RECORDS

If you have any employees, you must maintain careful records on them as well, including the following:

(a) Employment application

(b) Written reference verifications

(c) Verification of training, education, and experience

(d) Medical information

(e) Emergency contact persons

(f) Verification of criminal records check

(g) Verification of Child Abuse Registry check

(h) Training sessions attended

(i) Date employment began

(j) Termination date

These records must also be kept in strict confidence.

CHILD INFORMATION SHEET

Child's Name: _____

                                 First   Middle   Last

Name child goes by:_____

Address:_____Phone #_____

Date of Birth:_____   Age:_____

Parent/Guardian Name:_____

Address:_____Phone #_____

Parent/Guardian Name:_____

Address:_____Phone #_____

Mother's Employer:_____

Address:_____Phone #_____

Father's Employer:_____

Address:_____Phone #_____

Emergency Contact Person

1) Name:_____

Relationship:_____

Address:_____Phone #_____

2) Name:_____

Relationship:_____

Address:_____Phone #_____

Additional Persons who may pick up the child:

Name:_____

Relationship:_____

Name:_____

Relationship:_____

Physician's Name:_____

Address:_____Phone #_____

Comments: things we should know about your child; disabilities, hobbies, special interests, shyness, etc._____

_____

_____

_____

Proposed Date of Admission: _____

DATE: _____PARENT SIGNATURE:_____

PARENT SIGNATURE:_____

****

PLEASE DO NOT FILL IN THIS SECTION

Date of Admission to Care:_____
Date of Termination of Care:_____

Child's Progress:_____

_____

_____

_____

MEDICATION ADMINISTERED FORM

MEDICATION ADMINISTERED FORM

(to be attached to medication permission form)

Child's Name: _____

Name of medication:_____

Amount given:_____

Date medication began:_____

Date to be discontinued:_____

DAY	DATE	TIME	SIGNATURE

ACCIDENT, INJURY, AND ILLNESS REPORT

Child's Name: _____

Date:_____   Time of Accident:_____

Particulars of accident and injury:_____
_____
_____

Particulars of illness: (symptoms, treatment) _____
_____
_____

Type of aid administered:_____
_____
_____

Were the parents, guardian, and/or emergency contact person
notified?   YES _____   NO_____

Was hospital treatment required?   YES _____   NO _____

If yes, give particulars_____
_____
_____

Additional information, comments:_____
_____
_____
_____

DAILY INFORMATION FORM

PARENTS: Please complete this section.

Child's Name: _____

Date:_____   Time In:_____

BABY: Slept: _____ hours

Woke up at:_____ a.m.

Had a _____good_____restless_____night (please circle one)

If restless, what seemed to cause it? _____

_____(teething, fever, diarrhea)_____

Ate:_____   At:_____(time)

Drank: _____   At:_____(time)

Had a BM: YES _____NO_____

Any special requests for baby today? _____

_____

_____

Information we should be aware of? _____

_____

_____

****

Thank you - Have a great day!

CAREGIVER: Please complete this section.

BABY: Ate:_____for breakfast at: _____(time)
_____for snack (a.m.) _____
_____for lunch at: _____
_____for snack (p.m.)_____
Drank: _____Amount_____At:_____(time)
_____Amount:_____At_____
_____Amount:_____At:_____
_____Amount:_____At_____
Napped at:_____a.m. for:_____hours
at:_____p.m. for:_____hours
Had a BM at:_____stool was: _____
at: _____stool was:_____
at: _____stool was: _____
Baby's day was_____
_____
_____

Comments:_____
_____
_____

Baby Needs:_____
_____

London Bridge

This is a great game for four or more players.

Object of the game: to get caught and be swung to and fro.

How to play: two children are chosen to be the bridge; they stand facing each other with their hands held in an arch above their heads. The other children hold on to each others' waists and move under the bridge singing the song:

London Bridge is falling down,
Falling down, falling down,
London Bridge is falling down,
Falling down, falling down,
My fair lady.

When "lady" is sung, the two children being the bridge drop their arms and catch the child passing beneath them. They swing the prisoner back and forth while all the children sing:

Take the keys and lock her up,
Lock her up, lock her up,
Take the keys and lock her up,
My fair lady.

Again when "lady" is sung, the prisoner is set free to rejoin the group. The game continues until all the verses are sung (see below) or the children tire.

3rd verse — Build it up with iron and bars, iron and bars, iron and bars...

4th verse — Take the keys and lock her up...
5th verse — Iron bars will rust away...
6th verse — Take the keys...
7th verse — Build it up with silver and gold...
8th verse — Take the keys...
9th verse — Gold and silver I've not got...
10th verse – Take the keys...

17
CHILD ABUSE

a. YOUR RESPONSIBILITY TO REPORT ABUSE

Did you know that by law, you, as a child-care provider, are obligated to report cases of suspected child abuse? You are. As a matter of record, it is a criminal offense if you do not report such cases.

We, as adult members of society, have a responsibility to protect children; all children. It is our duty to report any suspected cases of child abuse or neglect. No matter how close we are to the child's parents, we must consider the child first for he or she is virtually incapable of doing anything in a situation such as this and his or her well-being may depend on our intervention.

Your work with children puts you in contact with many different parents and many different parenting styles. You'll see children cared for in many different ways and although you may not always agree with how a parent raises a child, you must respect it. But you cannot respect or condone a parent who neglects or physically, sexually, or emotionally abuses a child. You must report any suspicions you may have that a parent is mistreating a child.

b. WHAT CONSTITUTES ABUSE OR NEGLECT?

Abuse can be physical, sexual, or emotional. It is an act committed against a child.

Neglect is a failure by the parent to provide for the child's physical needs. It is an act of omission.

1. Physical abuse

Physical abuse is an act of violence that goes beyond the bounds of discipline. The resulting injuries may require medical attention or they may be less severe. Injuries as a result of abuse differ from normal childhood injuries in that they may be more frequent and affect parts of the body where usual injuries do not occur. Quite often, parents are at a loss to explain these injuries or in many cases act as though they are unaware of them.

2. Sexual abuse

Sexual abuse includes acts of incest, rape, intercourse, fondling, or exploiting a child. These acts may be committed by family members, relatives, friends, or strangers. This type of abuse often goes undetected because the child has been sworn to secrecy or threatened with violence if he or she tells.

3. Emotional abuse

Emotional abuse is a very serious weapon. It may consist of the parent undermining the child's self-image and self-confidence through humiliation, insults, criticism, or accusations. It may simply involve the parent depriving the child of love and affection, or ignoring the child altogether.

4. Neglect

Neglect is a failure of the parent to provide for the child's physical needs of food, clothing, and shelter, or the failure to provide adequate supervision and protection from danger.

c. SIGNS OF ABUSE OR NEGLECT

It is not always easy to detect child abuse nor is it always easy to distinguish between the bumps and scrapes of a normally active child and the signs of abuse. Look for the atypical bruises on the back of the child's thighs, the dislike of being touched or hugged, or the heavy discharge in a child's underpants to alert you to a potential problem.

Table #4 lists some major signs of abuse or neglect. A child who is in an abusive situation may display one or any number of these signs.

If you become suspicious of abuse —

(a) make notes,

(b) keep track of all unusual cuts, welts, and bruises;

(c) note changes in a child's manner and disposition, and

(d) when appropriate, question the child about physical problems. Note the answers and keep these as evidence for the authorities.

It may make you feel better about reporting the abuse when you have the evidence to back you up; however, a child with severe injuries or emotional distress should be reported right away.

Though you should be aware of the signs of abuse or neglect, you must not go out of your way to look for these signs in every child. You have to realize that bruises on a child's knees, shins, and elbows are typical signs of an active child, that some children are normally shy and tend to take their time warming up to strangers and new situations, and that some children are boisterous by nature.

d. THE ABUSIVE PARENT

Like the abused child, the abusive parent may demonstrate some standard characteristics. Typically, these parents may —

(a) have few friends and may not often associate with family members,

(b) be unable to explain their child's injuries and often appear to be unaware of them,

(c) not participate in parent meetings, family socials, or outside activities,

(d) overreact to your concerns about or problems with their child,

(e) constantly pick on the child,

(f) not trust anyone,

(g) not show affection towards the child,

(h) expect the child to be more than he or she is capable of being at their age,

(i) refuse to get medical care for their child's injuries or use a different hospital or clinic for each injury, and

(j) abuse drugs or alcohol.

Parents do not mean, for the most part, to abuse their children. There are many factors that play a role in their abusive behavior. Often a family is in a crisis, meaning there are marital problems, divorce proceedings, a death in the family, or financial difficulties. Often the abuser is unable to handle these situations and strikes out at the child. In other cases, the abuse is the result of having been a child of abuse themselves. These parents know no other way of dealing with their children. Drugs and alcohol may also play an extensive role in abuse and there are parents who are simply mentally or emotionally incapable of raising their children.

e. REPORTING ABUSE

It is never easy to report a parent, but it is your responsibility to protect the child. Even if your suspicions prove false, you have done the right thing by having them investigated. Reporting suspicions of abuse is the only way to protect the children and to get parents the help they need.

TABLE #4
SIGNS OF ABUSE OR NEGLECT

PHYSICAL ABUSE	EMOTIONAL ABUSE	SEXUAL ABUSE	NEGLECT
Unexplained cuts, welts, and bruises	Constant rocking, head banging, thumbsucking, biting	Difficulty in walking and/or sitting	Child is afraid of parents
Bruises on unusual parts of the body like the back, thighs, buttocks, and face	Trouble sleeping	Unusual vaginal discharge	Sores, bruises, welts or other injuries that appear to be untreated
An unusual number of cuts, bruises and welts	Withdrawn, unfriendly	Pain or itching in the child's private area	Child is unclean
Size and shape of the injury, i.e. bruises that are long like a belt strike	Seeks attention	Trouble in swallowing	Malnourished
Burns	Low self esteem	Trouble going to the bathroom	Child is left unsupervised
Fractures, dislocated joints	Bed-wetting	Withdrawal or reluctance to join in physical or outdoor activities	Show extremes in behavior like overly assertive and aggressive or very timid and withdrawn
Bite marks	Child whines, cries often	A knowledge of sex inappropriate for the age of the child	Has trouble learning or concentrating
	Show signs of regressive or excessive behavior		May seem almost mentally retarded
	Has trouble learning or concentrating		Dresses inappropriate for the weather
	May seem almost mentally retarded		
	Defiant		
	Speech Disorders		

The law says that you must report all suspicions of neglect or abuse. What do you do if you are concerned about a child's welfare?

(a) Call your local Children's Aid Society (Canada) or the children's services agency (United States), and tell them what you suspect. If you have kept notes on your suspicions, have these references handy.

(b) Remain calm and in control. You are doing what is right and have nothing to fear. Answer the agency's questions as best you can. If a child has told you outright that Mommy hit her with the belt or that Daddy plays with her privates, tell the agency exactly what the child has told you.

(c) In the case of a child who requires medical attention for his or her injuries, call the child's doctor immediately. Have the doctor report the findings.

The law protects the reporter of child abuse by allowing for total confidentiality (you are not required to give your name when reporting a case). It also provides you with complete immunity from civil or criminal liability should the report turn out to be untrue.

After your initial contact with the agency, a case worker will assess the situation by checking the agency's records to determine if the family is currently under investigation or if the parents or any family member is listed in their child abuse register as a result of former complaints, investigations, or convictions. If they feel your complaint is substantial and worthy of further investigation, they will assign a child protection worker or case worker to take the appropriate steps to interview the family, assess the extent of the abuse, and, if necessary, place the child in protective custody. All of this should take no longer than 48 hours.

If the agency does not contact you for a written report or to let you know the status of their investigation, you should contact them to see what has been done and if you can be of any further assistance, like providing continuing care for the child.

f. TELLING THE PARENTS

Your decision whether to tell the parent about your report will be a difficult one. It will depend on how well you know the parent, the circumstances surrounding the abuse, and if you think the parent will pull the child from your care where you cannot protect him or her. Of course, it also depends on your gut feelings about the whole situation.

You might want to consider the severity of the abuse when making your decision and the likelihood of a parent getting hostile towards you and the child if you mention the report. If you think any danger will come to the child, you might want to refrain from saying anything.

On the other hand, you might feel an obligation towards the parent to let him or her know that because of your concern for the child and because of your respect for the trying times the parent is going through (if that is the case), you thought it was best to seek help. You might explain that you had no choice because the law requires that you report all suspected cases of child abuse.

To help you with your decision as to whether to tell the parent, ask the person you contacted at the agency what he or she recommends and if he or she can give you suggestions on what to say or how to handle the situation.

Keep in mind that failing to report suspected cases of child abuse is like being an accessory to a crime. You knew what was going on but you did nothing to stop it. Don't let a parent's possible reaction to your report scare you off. It is the child's well-being that is at stake here. He or she needs your protection.

For more information on child abuse, visit your local library. Or, for 20¢ each, you can order the following information booklets from:

The Independent Order of Foresters
100 Border Ave.
Solana Beach, CA 92075

In Canada:
798 Don Mills Road
Don Mills, Ontario
M3C 1T9

- About Child Abuse
- About the Sexual Abuse of Children
- About Alcohol, Child Abuse, and Child Incest
- About Adults Abused As Children
- About Incest

The Independent Order of Foresters also has a variety of videos that deal with child abuse. Ask for the order sheet for a complete list of what is available.

Lunch and Dip

Carrot, celery, and cucumber sticks

Ham and cheese strips

Cored and seeded red and green peppers

Crackers

- Stuff carrot, celery and cucumber sticks into red pepper.

To make the dip you'll need:

½ cup creamy cottage cheese

¼ cup ranch dressing

Green onion

- Process ingredients for dip in blender or food processor until smooth; pour into green pepper.
- Put the red and green peppers on a large plate and arrange crackers and ham and cheese strips around them.

18

FINDING AND HIRING EMPLOYEES

Chances are that, if you are running a day care out of your home, you will not have the space to accommodate more children than you yourself can manage or are allowed to supervise under licensing regulations.

If, however, you do have the space to take in more children and you want to do so, you will be looking at hiring one or more staff members to assist you.

To assess your staffing needs, you'll want to refer to your licensing regulations. They will tell how many assistants you will need for the number of children you wish to take in.

a. WRITING A JOB DESCRIPTION

Before you can begin to advertise for help, you must have an understanding and description of the work you will be offering. A written job description will be invaluable when writing your help-wanted advertisement and it will help you weed through the list of applicants and save you time because you will only schedule interviews with those persons who meet the criteria you have outlined. Job descriptions, once formulated, should be kept on file for future reference.

The job description you outline should contain the following:

(a) Duties to be performed

(b) Education and special training required

(c) Any skills that will assist in performing the job well

(d) Hours the job entails

(e) Pay scale

b. RECRUITING EMPLOYEES

Placing an ad in your local newspaper for a child-care worker should generate a flood of phone calls or a pile of resumes, right? Well, not necessarily. Oh, you will get a good response rate, but these responses may not be from the type of employees you were hoping to find. After all, you need qualified, trained staff, not people who think caring for children is child's play.

Targeting your advertising ensures you of locating applicants who have the qualifications needed to properly staff your new center. To fill your roster sheet quickly, you need to advertise efficiently. Some of the best places to begin your search are —

(a) placement offices at community colleges and universities that offer early childhood education courses; some of these institutions maintain a list of graduates seeking teaching positions;

(b) child-care agencies, organizations, resource and referral services (local, state/provincial and national);

(c) vocational training centers that offer courses equivalent to ECE training; and

(d) community employment agencies.

Some of the best advertising ideas are —

(a) ads in student and neighborhood newspapers and in local, state/provincial and national child-care organization newsletters;

(b) notices posted on job boards at local, state/provincial, and national child-care organizations;

(c) placing flyers with information about your employment needs in student enrollment packages at colleges, universities, and vocational institutions (this is a great way to locate students, part-time and substitute staff, and keep your applications file filled with names to contact when you need to replace or hire new staff); and

(d) free advertising space (i.e., public service announcements, special calendar listings) in local newspapers or on local radio and television stations.

c. INTERVIEWING APPLICANTS

Getting the most out of an interview means having a list of questions that will elicit much information about the applicant, his or her philosophy, and his or her knowledge about child development and behavior.

Getting the most out of an interview also means knowing what you expect of or would like to see most in a future employee. Qualities such as congeniality, flexibility, and good communication skills can be as important as training, experience, and philosophy.

When interviewing, remember that questions that require direct yes or no responses do little to help you assess an applicant's qualifications, and they do not give you any insight into the person's knowledge of programming, activity planning, or discipline theories. These types of questions should be excluded from your interview questionnaire sheet.

Instead, ask open-ended questions like "What is the best thing a teacher can do for the children during free period?" or "How would you help a child, who is new to the center, adjust to his or her separation from the parent for the first time?" Pose scenarios — "What if...?" — and see how the applicant responds to a theoretical situation.

Also, be aware that certain types of questions are considered by law to be discriminatory and are not allowed. Do not ask questions about the applicant's race, religion, politics, family planning, or any other personal matters. Stick to questions directly pertinent to the skills needed for the job and you should be okay.

Try not to rush through an interview. Really get to know the person sitting across from you. Help him or her to relax, to feel comfortable enough to express opinions, theories, and qualifications without hesitation or intimidation. This is when you get to see the real person behind the mask of frightened apprehension. After all, to some people an interview seems like an interrogation by the Inquisition, and yet, this same applicant just might be the best person to care for your group of toddlers.

At the conclusion of the interview, thank the applicant for taking the time to chat with you. Let him or her know approximately when to expect to hear from you with regards to your decision. If you only plan to contact those you wish to hire, let the applicant know that. Never offer an applicant the job right away. You need time to check references, to verify educational background, and, most important, to reflect on the interview and how it compared to those of the other applicants.

For more on finding and hiring employees, see *A Small Business Guide to Employee Selection*, another title in the Self-Counsel Series.

d. TRIAL PERIOD

Once you have found the right person for your job, bring him or her in for a trial or probationary period that will allow you to determine if the employee is suited to your day care. Make sure the employee knows that he or she is on probation for the first few weeks and that if he or she does not fit in or work out for any reason you will not keep him or her on. You have too many people depending on you to keep someone on staff who does not compliment the goals and philosophy of your center. Don't keep anyone on your payroll who does not meet your standards.

e. BENEFITS AND INCENTIVES

The turnover rate in day care is often very high and one of the main reasons is low wages. High staff turnover is bad for your day care because of the costs and inconvenience of finding and training new people and because it is traumatic to the children to constantly have to bond with new caregivers. In addition, since your licensing requirements dictate how many staff you have to have for a given number of children, you cannot afford to be without necessary staff for even a day. So it is in your best interests to keep staff happy.

Obviously, you are going to pay them the best wages you can, but this may not be much compared to what they could earn in other jobs. The fact is, child-care employees at all levels are severely underpaid. You, as a business owner, have to do what you can with what you have, and sometimes that may mean finding innovative ways to keep your staff.

To encourage your staff to remain in your employ, you might want to give these ideas some thought:

(a) *Medical plans.* In Canada, all provinces have health plans that cover basic medical expenses. You could offer to pay all or part of your employees' provincial health insurance premiums. In the United States, however, medical insurance costs are extremely high. While you may find it expensive to subscribe to a plan, if it is possible to do so, offering employees a health care package would usually be the most appreciated benefit they could receive.

(b) *Dental plans.* These are also costly. However, they may prove to be a cheaper incentive than the higher wages you may not be able to afford.

(c) *Training allowances.* Employees who wish to continue their training in early childhood education or related courses should be encouraged to do so. Where finances allow, you could offer each employee an education allowance to help offset their schooling costs. Perhaps you might give them paid time off to attend these courses.

(d) *Recognition.* All employees like to feel appreciated. You could do special things for your staff, like hosting celebrations for course completion, giving theater tickets for birthdays, or providing a sincere pat on the back when a parent comments on their work or when you notice the great job they are doing. You can also let your staff know how much you value their work and their opinions by involving them in decisions that affect the day care. More important, let your staff know they can approach you at any time and not feel intimidated; that they can tell you their complaints; that you are accommodating. In other words, treat them as you would like to be treated — with respect.

(e) *Subsidized child care.* An employee with a child in your day care will have one more reason to stay with you. Encourage employees with children to bring them into your day care by subsidizing their fees by a certain amount.

There are many other innovative ways to compensate an employee and ensure loyalties. Talk to other day-care operators. Find out what their personnel policies are, then look for ways that you can afford to make your business a more appealing place to work. Remember, though, your main priority is to give your staff the remuneration they deserve. Sometimes that may mean tightening purse strings on needless spending or a complete review of your budget.

Whatever incentives you decide to include in your personnel policy, put them in writing and give a copy of this policy to your applicants to review during the interview. While you are deciding whether you want to hire a certain applicant, he or she is also deciding whether or not they actually want to work for you. Tip the scales in your favor whenever possible.

For more on employee incentive programs, see *Motivating Today's Work Force*, another title in the Self-Counsel Series.

What Time Is It, Mr. Wolf?

This game works well with four or more players.

Object of the game: not to get caught by the Wolf.

How to play: One child is the Wolf. The Wolf stands across the room or across the field from the other children with his or her back turned away from them. The children ask "What time is it, Mr. Wolf?" The Wolf replies, "One o'clock," or any time he or she wishes. Whatever time the Wolf says, the children take that number of steps away from the wall. This continues till the Wolf says "Lunch time!" and chases the children back to the other side. Those who are caught have to line up with the Wolf until everyone else is caught. The last one caught gets to be the new Wolf.

19
THE OUT-OF-HOME DAY CARE

This chapter is for those of you whose ambitions reach beyond a home-based day care with a few children. Much of the information given in previous chapters is applicable whether you are planning to accommodate 2 children or 20. If you are planning to open a larger day-care center, you will simply be working on a larger scale. The information given here, however, is geared specifically to the out-of-home day care.

a. WHAT KIND OF DAY CARE DO YOU WANT TO OPERATE?

One of your first decisions is how many children of what ages you want to care for.

The number of children you can accommodate in your center will be dictated by the size of the facilities you will be renting or buying. Licensing regulations will specify the area needed for each child in the center. You can, of course, choose to rent a larger or smaller space, depending on the type of business you want to run. Are you thinking of a small, intimate center with perhaps 15 children and a few workers, or does the challenge of organizing and running a large-scale operation appeal to you? Decide how big you want to be and then find facilities to fit that size.

You must also decide what age(s) of children you prefer to work with. Will you accept a variety of ages and the accompanying expense of a variety of toys and equipment, or concentrate on certain age groups? For example, some centers do not accept infants. These centers may work with a number of home day cares that provide care for infants until they are old enough to move into the center. Other centers offer before- and after-school care for the kindergarten-plus age group, bringing in extra staff at those hours to accommodate these children.

If you have volunteered your time at other centers, you'll have a pretty good idea of the size of the center you want to operate as well as the ages of the children with whom you prefer to work. If not, perhaps now is a good time to visit a few centers. Get a feel for their programs. If you find one that suits you, talk to the operator or director, and ask their advice on how you can set up a similar operation.

In order for you to maintain quality child care, you need a good cash flow, which means reaching and maintaining full capacity with respect to the number of children your license allows. For those of you who are uncertain as to the numbers and ages of the children you are capable of working with, it is advisable to start out slowly, caring for only a few children at the beginning and adding new children and staff only when you feel confident about doing so.

b. FINDING A LOCATION

There is a lot to think about when you are shopping around for the perfect place to set up shop. It's like buying clothes. The place has to have just the right appeal, fit exactly to your measurements, and have enough room for you to move around in, all at a price you can afford. When you have done your needs assessment (see Sample #1), you will know in what general area you should start looking. Your next step is locating the right facility, building, or parcel of land on which to build, if finances allow.

For hints about sites which will soon be vacant, contact your regional housing or building authority responsible for maintaining lists of available buildings. Drive or walk through the area you are interested in. Note any buildings that appeal to you, then call the housing authority to inquire about possible vacancies.

Keep in mind that the ideal location for child care has an adjoining outside play area and is preferably a single-level building. Houses can be ideal locations as the kitchen and washroom facilities are already installed. Also, old schools with plumbing, wiring, and heating systems in good shape make for great centers.

Another idea you could consider is to rent from or share space with a church or Sunday school, community or civic center. In some areas where day care is badly needed, a church, synagogue, or civic organization may be willing to donate the space. It is an avenue worth pursuing.

Yet another idea is to talk to the administration at the local hospital, factory, or industrial complex about establishing an on-site facility that would enable parents to spend time with their children on their lunch breaks, and would also help lower absentee rates when parents have trouble with their child-care arrangements. If an on-site center is not possible, these businesses may be willing to help with your start-up costs if you establish a facility nearby.

When a realtor or landlord takes you on a tour of the building, use a checklist to make notes on the suitability of the facility (see Worksheet #15).

A word of caution at this point. DO NOT SIGN any lease or purchase agreement until you have had time to review zoning, health, sanitation, and fire reports.

c. LEGAL LEGWORK

Once you find a building or space that satisfies your criteria, the next step will be to consult a lawyer to look into the legal aspects of your purchase or lease and to investigate local zoning ordinances and/or home-owner/property-owner agreements that may prohibit the establishment of your day care.

Zoning is the regulation of land use by local planners. In some cases, these laws can be changed or declared less restrictive. Your lawyer will be able to discuss this with you.

You will find, in most cases, the application to operate a day-care center must be accompanied by the following:

(a) A report from the health officer for your municipality with regard to the sanitation, lighting, ventilation, and general health and safety of the facility

(b) A report from the fire commissioner regarding the fire safety standards of the facility

(c) A proposed operating budget for the year

(d) Information about the zoning of the property on which the facility will operate

(e) A floor plan in detail of the facility showing the measurements of the facility and the location of any fixed equipment in it

In some states and provinces you will also need:

(a) A recent authorized medical statement showing the results of your tuberculin test, and your physician's opinion of your mental and emotional health capability for such a job

WORKSHEET #15
LOCATION CHECKLIST

QUESTION	YES	NO	CAN IMPROVE
1. Is the building easily accessible via major traffic arteries and is there a bus route nearby?			
2. Are there adequate parking facilities for parents?			
3. Is the building in a good location for children to play?			
4. Is there a park close by?			
5. Is there ample space to set up an outdoor play area?			
6. Is the outdoor area fenced?			
7. Is the building appealing and well maintained with — (a) adequate heating (b) good plumbing, and (c) an up-to-code electrical system?			
8. Is the space you are interested in on the main floor?			
9. Is the interior of the building well maintained?			
10. Is the building spacious and does it allow for good floor planning?			
11. Is the entrance to the building and the space you want to rent open enough to allow room for parents and children to move around in?			
12. Are there washrooms nearby?			
13. Are the walls soundproof?			
14. Are the rooms well–lit?			
15. Is there an abandance of windows for both sunlight and fire escapes?			
16. Will the landlord allow major renovations?			
17. Is the landlord willing to offset some of these renovation costs; e.g., paint, lighting, flooring, general upgrading?			

(b) References who can attest to your character

So, get that pen and paper handy, call city hall, and find out the names and numbers of —

(a) the health officer,

(b) the fire commissioner,

(c) the zoning officer, and

(d) the sanitation officer.

Then work through the following procedure:

(a) Get the zoning regulations from city hall, review them carefully or pass them on to your lawyer for review. If there is not a problem with locating a day care where you are interested, proceed with number two. If zoning restrictions forbid the operating of such a facility, discuss obtaining a variance with your lawyer.

(b) Call the landlord or real estate agent to find out when you can schedule the fire, health, and sanitation inspections.

(c) Set up appointments with the fire commissioner and the health and sanitation officers to inspect the building .

(d) Meet with these officials, if possible, to find out what needs to be done to bring the building up to code. Find out when you can expect their written reports.

If all goes well, you will have passed all your inspections and can let out a sigh of relief and carry on with your plans. But life is not always fair. Perhaps the reports came back saying the building needs improvements. You will have to decide at this point if the improvements are worth your investment.

You are a businessperson now, an entrepreneur. You have to make decisions and work within your budget. This may be the first hard decision you will have to make. Be firm. Contact a few contractors and get estimates on the renovations necessary to meet all standards. Then weigh the feasibility of going ahead with these renovations.

If you've got your heart set on the building you've found because the area is clean and well-cared for or it has all the amenities close at hand, talk to your landlord. Find out if he or she is willing to bring the building up to code or if he or she will split the costs. When a purchase agreement comes into play, figure the costs of improvements into your purchase price and reduce the price accordingly. In the event it's just too big and expensive a job for you to concern yourself with, walk away and look somewhere else. It's as simple as that.

d. THE DIRECTOR OF YOUR CENTER

When you run a home day care, you are both the owner/operator of the day care and the director. But if you open a larger center, this will not necessarily be the case. You may be more interested in the business side and want to concentrate on operating the center, or you may not feel you want to direct the day-to-day programming of 40 children.

If you decide that you will be the director of your own center, remember that you must still qualify in training experience and educational background according to the licensing regulations. All persons assuming the position of day-care director must be approved by the licensing board.

If, on the other hand, you want to hire someone for this role, you will be entrusting the success of your center to this person's abilities, so consider your candidates carefully.

You or your director will be responsible for the following:

(a) Daily operation and management of the center and its programs

(b) Program development

(c) Outlining the training of staff

(d) Maintaining the center's goals and philosophy

(e) Ensuring the safety and well-being of the children

(f) Parent involvement and education

(g) Maintaining licensing standards

(h) Hiring, scheduling, and supervising staff

(i) Budgeting

(j) Facility maintenance for hygiene, safety, and appearance

The person you hire should have a minimum of a bachelor's degree in early childhood education or equivalent, such as high school diploma and four years' experience in child care. He or she should have a minimum of two years' experience supervising the age group your center caters to. Your director should also have taken at least one course in administration. He or she should have a comprehension of —

(a) curriculum planning,

(b) child development,

(c) child health and nutrition,

(d) business management,

(e) employee relations,

(f) good communication,

(g) first aid and CPR, and

(h) community resources.

When is the best time to hire a director or administrator? Hopefully a good few months before you open your doors to provide care. There are many reasons for this, but mainly you will need someone to assist you with your pre–opening work load. The tasks of the director might include the following:

(a) Assisting with program and policies development

(b) Preparing budgets

(c) Developing written job descriptions

(d) Assisting with interviewing and hiring staff

(e) Assisting with the purchase of equipment and supplies

(f) Locating available sources of funding and writing the necessary proposals to secure the funding

e. OTHER STAFF

Other staff members might include —

(a) child-care teachers,

(b) assistant teachers,

(c) substitute teachers,

(d) volunteers, and

(e) support staff (e.g., cook, caretaker, bookkeeper).

Table #5 lists these positions, their job descriptions, and the qualifications necessary to perform them.

In addition, each member of your staff must possess the following:

(a) Physician's note stating the physical and mental capability of the applicant to handle child-care work and that he or she is free of infectious disease

(b) Current results of a tuberculosis test and chest x-ray

(c) Fingerprint clearance

When you are planning schedules for your staff, remember the following points:

(a) Somewhere in your licensing regulations are words to the effect: **Under no circumstances is a child to be left un–supervised. Students and volunteers do not qualify as supervisory staff. A teacher or assistant teacher must be present at all times in the room where children are being cared for.**

(b) The director and/or his or her consignee must be available and in the building at all times.

(c) A teacher or assistant teacher assigned to a group must not be involved in any other activities except that of providing care. When an employee is responsible for other duties (i.e., cooking, cleaning), another teacher must be assigned to take over the duty of supervising the group.

(d) As primary caregiver for an individual group, the teacher or assistant teacher must be with the same group for a guaranteed number of hours per day to allow the children to bond with a particular caregiver.

TABLE #5
STAFF RESPONSIBILITIES AND QUALIFICATIONS

POSITIONS	RESPONSIBILITIES	EDUCATION	SKILLS AND TRAITS
Child-care teacher	Cares for and supervises groups of children Assists the director in planning and implementing the program Supervises assistants, substitutes, and volunteers Fills out daily reports Attends staff meetings Acts as director on occasion	1-year ECE certificate or equivalent High school diploma or child development credential or 3 years experience in child care Current first aid and CPR certificate	Good understanding of child development and program planning Good communication skills Able to supervise both large and small groups Able to supervise other staff Warm Responsible Flexible and Cheerful
Assistant teacher	Assists with groups of children Acts as primary caregiver for smaller groups Implements activities as outlined in program Attends staff meetings Participates in training sessions and continues ECE training	In training for ECE certificate or has completed a recognized training course equivalent to 1 year of ECE Some experience in child care Current first aid and CPR certificate	Good understanding of child development Able to supervise small groups Warm Responsible Flexible and Cheerful
Substitute teacher	Understands and implements the program for the group they care for	Qualified as per individual licensing requirements	As above
Volunteer	Meets personal and health requirements Visits the center regularly to become familiar with programs and policies	None	Genuinely interested in children Warm and affectionate
Support Staff	Carries out duties appropriate to the position	Education appropriate to the position	Open and friendly with children

187

APPENDIX 1
GOVERNMENT OFFICES

a. UNITED STATES

Alabama Department of Human Resources
50 North Ripley Street
Montgomery, Alabama 36130
(205)-261-5360

Department of Health and Social Services
Division of Family and Youth Services
230 South Franklin Street, Suite 206
Juneau, Alaska 99801
(907)-465-3013

Arizona Department of Health Services
Office of Children
Day Care Facilities Division
100 West Clerdon Street, 4th Floor
Phoenix, Arizona 85013
(602)-255-1272

Division of Children and Family Services
Day Care Licensing Division
P.O. Box 1437
Little Rock, Arkansas 72203
(501)-682-8590

Community Care Licensing
Department of Social Services
Day Care Unit
744 P Street, Mail Station 19-50
Sacramento, California 95814
(916)-324-4031

Department of Social Services
Day Care Unit
605 Bannock Street, Room 354
Denver, Colorado 80204
(303)-893-7166

Community Nursing Home Health Division
Child Day Care Licensing Unit
141 - 150 Washington Street
Hartford, Connecticut 06106
(203)-566-2575

Licensing Bureau
Delaware Youth and Family Center
1825 Faulkland Road
Wilmington, Delaware 19805-1195
(302)-633-2695

Licensing and Certification Division
Social Services Branch
614 H Street, N.W., Room 1031
Washington, DC 20001
(202)-727-7226

Office of Children, Youth and Family
Department of Health and
    Rehabilitation Services
1317 Winewood Boulevard
Tallahassee, Florida 32399
(904)-488-4900

Child Care Licensing Office,
Room 607
Department of Human Resources
878 Peachtree Street, N.E.
Atlanta, Georgia 30309
(404)-894-5688

Department of Human Services,
Licensing Unit
420 Weiaka Milo Road, Suite 101
Honolulu, Hawaii 96817-4941
(808)-832-5025

Department of Health and Welfare
Family and Children's Division
4355 Emerald Street, 2nd Floor
Boise, Idaho 83706
(208)-334-6800

Department of Children and
    Family Services
406 East Munro Avenue
Springfield, Illinois 62701-1498
(217)-785-2598

State of Indiana
Department of Public Welfare
Child Welfare/Social Service Division
402 West Washington Street, Room W364
Indianapolis, Indiana 46204
(317)-232-4440

Division of Adult, Children and
  Family Services
Iowa Department of Human Services
Hoover State Office Building
Des Moines, Iowa 50319
(515)-281-6074

Kansas Department of Health
  and Environment
Landon State Office Building
Child Care Licensing Section
900 S.W. Jackson Street
Topeka, Kansas 66612-1290
(913)-296-1275

Division of Licensing and Regulation
Cabinet for Human Resources Building
Fourth Floor East
Frankfort, Kentucky 40621
(502)-564-2800

Department of Social Services
Department of Health and Hospitals
P.O. Box 3767/P.O. Box 3078
Baton Rouge, Louisiana 70821
(504)-342-6446

Department of Human Services
Bureau of Child and Family Services
221 State Street
Augusta, Maine 04333
(207)-289-5060

Office of Licensing and Certification
Division of Child Care Centers
4201 Patterson Avenue
Baltimore, Maryland 21215
(301)-764-2750

Office for Children
10 West Street
Boston, Massachusetts 02111
(617)-727-8956

Division of Child Day Care Licensing
Michigan Department of Social Services
235 South Grand Street, Suite 1212
P.O. Box 30037
Lansing, Michigan 48909
(517)-373-8300

Department of Human Services
Division of Licensing
444 LaFayette Road
Street Paul, Minnesota 55155-3842
(612)-296-3971

Division of Child Care and Special Licensure
Mississippi State Department of Health
P.O. Box 1700
Jackson, Mississippi 39215-1700
(601)-960-7504

State Department of Social Services
Division of Family Services
State Office of Child Care
Licensing Unit
P.O. Box 88
Jefferson City, Missouri 65103
(314)-751-2450

Department of Family Services
P.O. Box 8005
Helena, Montana 59604
(406)-444-5900

Department of Social Services
P.O. Box 95026
301 Centennial Mall South, 5th Floor
Lincoln, Nebraska 68509-5062
(402)-471-3121

Bureau of Services for Child Care
505 East King Street, Room 101
Carson City, Nevada 89710
(702)-687-5911

Division of Public Health Services
Bureau of Child Care Standards
  and Licensure
Health and Human Services Building
6 Hazen Drive
Concord, New Hampshire 03301
(603)-271-4624

Bureau of Licensing
Division of Youth and Family Services
CN 717
Trenton, New Jersey 08625-0717
(609)-292-9220

Licensing Health-Related Facilities
Public Health Division
1190 Street Francis Drive
Santa Fe, New Mexico 87503
(505)-827-2389

Bureau of Daycare Licensing
65 Worth Street, 4th Floor
New York, New York 10013
(212)-334-7803

Office of Child Day Care Licensing
Child Day Care Section
701 Barbour Drive
Raleigh, North Carolina 27603
(919)-733-4801

North Dakota Department of
Human Services
Children and Family Services Division
Judicial Wing, 3rd Floor
600 East Boulevard Avenue
Bismarck, North Dakota 58505-0250
(701)-224-3580

Office of Child Care Services
30 East Broad Street, 30th Floor
Columbus, Ohio 43266-0423
(614)-466-3822

Department of Human Services
Child Care Licensing Unit
P.O. Box 25352
Oklahoma City, Oklahoma 73125
(405)-521-3561

Department of Human Resources
Children's Services Division
198 Commercial Street S.E.
Salem, Oregon 97310
(503)-378-3178

Pennsylvania Department of Public Welfare
Central Region Day Care Services
P.O. Box 2675
Lanco Lodge Building 25
Harrisburg, Pennsylvania 17105
(717)-787-8691

Department of Children and Their Families
Day Care Licensing Unit
610 Mount Pleasant Ave., Building 2
Providence, Rhode Island 02908
(401)-457-4708

South Carolina Department of Social Services
Day Care Licensing Division
P.O. Box 1520
Columbia, South Carolina 29202-1520
(803)-734-5740

Department of Social Services
Child Protection Services
Richard F. Kneip Building
700 Governor's Drive
Pierre, South Dakota 57501-2291
(605)-773-3227

Day Care Licensing Division
Tennessee Department
   of Human Services
1000 Second Avenue
P.O. Box 1135
Nashville, Tennessee 37202
(615)-244-9706

Texas Department of Human Services
Day Care Licensing Division
P.O. Box 149030, W-403
Austin, Texas 78714-9030
(512)-450-3261

Division of Human Services
Office of Licensing
120 North 200 West
Salt Lake City, Utah 84145
(801)-538-4242

Licensing and Regulations Division
Day Care Unit
Department of Social and
   Rehabilitation Services
103 South Main Street
Waterbury, Vermont 05676
(802)-241-2158

Division of Licensing Programs
Department of Social Services,
Suite 219
8007 Discovery Drive, Tyler Building
Richmond, Virginia 23239
(804)-662-9025

Department of Social and Health Services
Division of Children and Family Services
P.O. Box 45710
Olympia, Washington 98504
(206)-586-2688

West Virginia Department of
Human Resources
Office of Social Services
Building 6, Room 850
Charleston, West Virginia 25305
(304)-348-7980

Day Care Licensing
Department of Health and Social Services
3601 Memorial Drive
Madison, Wisconsin 43704
(608)-249-0441

Division of Public Assistance and
    Social Services
Family Services Unit
Hathaway Building, 3rd Floor
Cheyenne, Wyoming 82002
(307)-777-7561

b. CANADA

Day Care Programs
Alberta Family and Social Services
11th Floor, 7th Street Plaza
10030 - 107th Street
Edmonton, Alberta
T5J 3E4
(403)-427-4477

Support Services Division
Ministry of Social Services
3rd Floor, 614 Humboldt Street
Victoria, British Columbia
V8V 1X4
(604)-387-6213

Child Care Branch
Ministry of Women's Equality
Government of British Columbia
3rd Floor, 756 Fort Street
Victoria, British Columbia
V8V 1X4
(604)-356-7910

Manitoba Child Day Care
Department of Family Services
2nd Floor, 114 Garry Street
Winnipeg, Manitoba
R3C 1G1
(204)-945-2197
1-800-282-8069

Office for Childhood Services
Department of Health and
    Community Services
P.O. Box 5100
Fredericton, New Brunswick
E3B 5G8
(506)-453-2950

Day Care and Homemaker Services
Department of Social Services
3rd Floor, Confederation Building,
West Block
St. John's, Newfoundland
A1B 4J6
(709)-729-3590

Child Day Care Program
Department of Social Services
Government of Northwest Territories
500 - 4920 - 52nd Street
Yellowknife, Northwest Territories
X1A 3T1
(403)-920-8920

Day Care Services
Family and Children's Services Division
Department of Community Services
P.O. Box 696
Halifax, Nova Scotia
B3J 2T7
(902)-424-3204

Child Care Branch
Ministry of Community and Social Services
30th Floor, 2 Bloor Street West
Toronto, Ontario
M7A 1E9
(416)-327-4855

Early Childhood Services
Department of Health and
Social Services
P.O. Box 2000
Charlottetown, Prince Edward Island
C1A 7N8
(902)-368-4957

Office des services de garde a l'enfance
100, rue Sherbrooke est
Montreal, Quebec
H2X 1C3
(514)-873-2323
1-800-363-0310

Child Day Care Division
Department of Social Services
11th Floor, 1920 Broad Street
Chateau Towers
Regina, Saskatchewan
S4P 3V6
(306)-787-3855

Child Care Services Unit
Department of Health and
 Social Services
Government of Yukon
Box 2703
Whitehorse, Yukon Territory
Y1A 2C6
(403)-667-3492

APPENDIX 2
CHILD CARE ORGANIZATIONS AND ASSOCIATIONS

a. UNITED STATES

National Association for the Education
  of Young Children (NAEYC)
1834 Connecticut Avenue N.W.
Washington, D.C. 20009-5786
(202)-232-8777
1-800-424-2460

National Association of Child Care
Resource and Referral Agencies
2116 Campus Drive S.E.
Rochester, Minnesota 55904
(507)-287-2220

Child Care Action Campaign
330 Seventh Avenue, 17th Floor
New York, New York 10001
(212)-239-0138

The Child Care Employee Project
6536 Telegraph Avenue, Suite A-201
Oakland, California 94609-1114
(510)-653-9889

Children's Defense Fund
122 C Street N.W.
Washington, D.C. 20001
(202)-628-8787
1-800-424-9602

National Black Child
Development Institute
1463 Rhode Island Avenue, N.W.
Washington, D.C. 20005
(202)-387-1281

National Association for
Family Day Care
15153 Gramercy Drive
Clifton Heights, Pennsylvania 19018
(215)-622-0663

Child Care Law Center
22 Second Street, 5th Floor
San Francisco, California 94105
(415)-495-5498

b. CANADA

Canadian Child Care Federation
120 Holland,
Suite 401
Ottawa, Ontario
K1Y 0X6
(613)-729-5289

Childcare Resource and Research Unit
Centre for Urban and Community Studies
University of Toronto
455 Spadina Avenue, #406
Toronto, Ontario
M5S 2G8
(416)-978-6895

Child Care Programs
6th Floor, Brooke Claxton Building
Tunney's Pasture
Ottawa, Ontario
K1A 1B5
(613)-957-0611

Canadian Association of
Toy Libraries and Resource Centres
120 Holland Avenue, #205
Ottawa, Ontario
K1Y 0X6
(613)-729-5421

Canadian Association for Young Children
252 Bloor Street W., Suite 12-115
Toronto, Ontario
M5S 1V5
(604)-926-6999

BIBLIOGRAPHY

Baker, Katherine Read. *Let's Play Outdoors*. Washington, D.C.: National Association For The Education of Young Children, 1987.

Bellm, Dan, and Marcy Whitebook. *A Good Sub is Hard to Find*. Berkeley, CA: Child Care Employee Project, 1989.

Campbell, Sheila D., Ph.D. *Facilities and Equipment for Day Care Centers*. Ottawa, Ontario: Health and Welfare Canada, 1984.

Cataldo, Christine Z. *Infant and Toddler Programs*. Reading, MA: Addison-Wesley, 1982.

Children With Special Needs. Ottawa: Health and Welfare Canada, 1990.

Cleveland, Gordon, Martha Friendly, Tricia Willis, and Sonia Ostrowska. *Assessing Child Care Needs: Sample Questionnaires*. Toronto: The Center for Urban and Community Studies, 1990.

Collins, Raymond C. "Child care and the States: The Comparative Licensing Study." *Young Children: The Journal of the National Association for the Education of Young Children*. National Association for the Education of Young Children, Washington, D.C.: 1976.

Dunster, Lee. *Family Daycare: A Caregiver's Guide*. Ottawa: Child Care Providers Association, 1990.

Endsley, Richard C., and Marilyn R. Bradbard. *Quality Day Care*. Englewood Cliffs, NJ: Prentice-Hall, Inc., 1981.

Family Communications. *Mister Roger's Plan and Play Book*. Pittsburgh, PA: Family Communications, 3rd edition, 1991.

Feeney, Stephanie, and Joan M. Zeller. *Toys: Tools for Learning*. Washington, D.C.: National Association for the Education of Young Children, 1990 .

Friendly, Martha. *Assessing Community Need for Child Care*. Toronto: The Centre for Urban and Community Studies, 1989.

Galinsky, Ellen, and William H. Hooks. *The New Extended Family: Daycare That Works*. Boston, MA: Houghton Mifflin Company, 1977.

Good Books For a Good Start. Ottawa: Health and Welfare Canada, 1991.

Goodwin, Annabelle, and Lorraine Schrag, eds. *Setting Up for Infant Care*. Washington, D.C.: National Association For The Education Of Young Children, 1992.

Guidelines for Appropriate Curriculum Content and Assessment in Programs Serving Children Ages 3 Through 8. Washington, D.C.: National Association for the Education of Young Children, 1990.

Initial Steps in Starting a Day Nursery in Ontario. Toronto: Ontario Ministry of Community and Social Services, 1991.

Kennedy, Daniel S. *The Ultimate Marketing Plan*. Holbrook, MA: Bob Adams, 1991.

Lande, Jeffrey S., and Sandra Scarr, eds. *Caring for Children, Challenge to America*. Hillsdale, NJ: Lawrence Erlbaum Associates, 1989.

McCracken, Janet Brown. *Keeping Healthy*. Washington, D.C.: National Association for the Education of Young Children, 1990.

Modigliani, Kathy, Marianne Reiff, and Sylvia Jones. *Opening Your Door to Children*. Washington, D.C.: National Association For The Education of Young Children, 1991.

National Statement on Quality Child Care. Ottawa: Canadian Child Care Federation, 1991.

Ohio Office of Child Care Services. *Child Abuse and Neglect*. Columbus, OH: Ohio Department of Human Services, 1987.

Rhodes, Greg, and Cheri Sterman. *Caring for Children in Your Home*. Columbus, OH: Ohio Department of Human Services, 1987.

OTHER TITLES IN THE
SELF-COUNSEL BUSINESS SERIES

PREPARING A SUCCESSFUL BUSINESS PLAN

A practical guide for small business
by Rodger Touchie, B.Comm., M.B.A.

At some time, every business needs a formal business plan. Whether considering a new business venture or rethinking an existing one, an effective plan is essential to success. From start to finish, this working guide outlines how to prepare a plan that will win potential investors and help achieve business goals.

Using worksheets and a sample plan, readers learn how to create an effective plan, establish planning and maintenance methods, and update their strategy in response to actual business conditions. $14.95

Contents include:

- The basic elements of business planning
- The company and its product
- The marketing plan
- The financial plan
- The team
- Concluding remarks and appendixes
- The executive summary
- Presenting an impressive document
- Common misconceptions in business planning
- Your business plan as a tangible asset

BASIC ACCOUNTING FOR THE SMALL BUSINESS

Simple, foolproof techniques for keeping your books straight and staying out of trouble
by Clive Cornish, C.G.A.

Having bookkeeping problems? Do you feel you should know more about bookkeeping, but simply don't have time for a course? Do you wish that the paperwork in your business could be improved, but you don't know where or how to start?

This book is a down-to-earth manual on how to save your accountant's time and your time and money. Written in clear, everyday English, not in accounting jargon, this guide will help you and your office staff keep better records.

Inside you will find illustrations of sample forms and instructions on how to prepare all the records you will need to keep, including:

- Daily cash sheet
- Cash summary
- Statement ledger
- Payables journal
- Synoptic journal
- Payroll book
- Income statement
- Trial balance
- Columnar work sheet

U.S. ed. $7.95, Canadian ed. $8.95

GETTING PUBLICITY

A do-it-yourself guide for small business and non-profit groups

by Tana Fletcher and Julia Rockler, B.A.

If you dream of getting publicity for your business, your organization, or yourself, you need this book. Step-by-step instructions illustrate just what it takes to attract media attention to any enterprise. The authors, both award-winning journalists, show how to make the most of every opportunity for free coverage in the print and broadcast media and how to handle the resulting interviews with ease.

Regardless of your budget or your background, with this book you can learn how to sparkle in the media spotlight. Aimed specifically at individuals and organizations whose ambitions are bigger than their bankrolls, *Getting Publicity* emphasizes low-cost, do-it-yourself promotional strategies. Filled with inexpensive and practical tips for capitalizing on the power of publicity, this comprehensive guide includes suggestions on everything from preparing press kits to appearing on television. In addition, several advanced publicity skills are simplified, including how to become a sought-after speaker, when to hold a news conference, and why it's important to maintain positive media relationships. $12.95

Contents include:

- How to prepare your publicity materials for maximum impact
- Who to contact in the media

ORDER FORM

All prices are subject to change without notice. Books are available in book, department, and stationery stores. If you cannot buy the book through a store, please use this order form. (Please print)

Name _____

Address _____

_____

Charge to: ❑ Visa   ❑ MasterCard

Account Number _____

Validation Date _____

Expiry Date_____

Signature_____

❑ **Check here for a free catalogue.**

IN CANADA
Please send your order to the nearest location:
Self-Counsel Press
1481 Charlotte Road
North Vancouver, B. C.
V7J 1H1

Self-Counsel Press
8-2283 Argentia Road
Mississauga, Ontario
L5N 5Z2

IN THE U.S.A.
Please send your order to:
Self-Counsel Press Inc.
1704 N. State Street
Bellingham, WA 98225

YES, please send me:

_____copies of **Preparing a Successful Business Plan**, $14.95

_____copies of **Basic Accounting for the Small Business** U.S. $7.95 Canadian, $8.95

_____copies of **Getting Publicity**, $12.95

Please add $2.50 for postage & handling.
Canadian residents, please add 7% GST to your order.
WA residents, please add 7.8% sales tax.